The Prophesied Coming of Christ

Phyllis Carol Olive

The Prophesied Coming of Christ

Book of Mormon, Native America, and Latter-day Prophecies of the Second Coming

CFI, an imprint of Cedar Fort, Inc.
Springville, Utah

ISBN 13: 978-1-4621-2050-5

Published by CFI, an imprint of Cedar Fort, Inc., 2373 W. 700 S., Springville, UT 84663
Distributed by Cedar Fort, Inc., www.cedarfort.com

LIBRARY OF CONGRESS CATALOGING-IN-PUBLICATION DATA

Names: Olive, Phyllis Carol, author.
Title: The prophesied coming of Christ : Book of Mormon, native America, and latter-day prophecies of the Second Coming / Phyllis Carol Olive.
Description: Springville, Utah : CFI, an Imprint of Cedar Fort, Inc., [2017] | Includes bibliographical references and index.
Identifiers: LCCN 2017003796 (print) | LCCN 2017006584 (ebook) | ISBN 9781462120505 (pbk. : alk. paper) | ISBN 9781462128051
Subjects: LCSH: Second Advent. | End of the world. | Church of Jesus Christ of Latter-day Saints--Doctrines. | Mormon Church--Doctrines.
Classification: LCC BX8643.E83 O45 2017 (print) | LCC BX8643.E83 (ebook) | DDC 236/.9--dc23
LC record available at https://lccn.loc.gov/2017003796

Cover design by Kinsey Beckett

Edited and typeset by Chelsea Holdaway

Printed in the United States of America

10 9 8 7 6 5 4 3 2 1

Printed on acid-free paper

Contents

Preface

America's Coming Storm

There can be little doubt that we live in troubled times. Prophets throughout history have prophesied of our day, each of them speaking of the dire conditions that humanity would face at the end of the world prior to the Lord's prophesied Second Coming. Numerous books have been written on this subject—each calling for humanity to be prepared against the events destined to cleanse the world of its wickedness before the days of the Lord. This book will be no different, except it will include the prophecies of the various prophets of the Book of Mormon and even some of the Lamanite descendants of Lehi, for they too are of Israel and have been promised continued existence in the land. We learn of their place in Israel right on the title page of the Book of Mormon, which states the following:

> The Book of Mormon, An Account Written by the Hand of Mormon upon Plates Taken from the Plates of Nephi.
>
> *Wherefore, it is an abridgment of the record of the people of Nephi and also of the Lamanites—Written to the Lamanites, who are a remnant of the house of Israel; and also to the Jew and Gentile—Written by way of commandment, and also by the spirit of prophecy and of revelation.* (Book of Mormon title page; emphasis added)

The Book of Mormon makes it clear that the Nephites knew of Jesus Christ long before His appearance to the faithful after His death and Resurrection. Prophets among them even prophesied of His ultimate

Second Coming at the end of the world. Thanks to the Bible, the Gentiles were also made aware of their Savior and the prophesied Second Coming. Yet, it is through the Book of Mormon that we learn of the sacred nature of America—it being the place of the New Jerusalem—the place where the Savior will rule for a thousand years of peace. The Jaredite prophet Ether said,

> 5 And he spake also concerning the house of Israel, and the Jerusalem from whence Lehi should come—after it should be destroyed it should be built up again, a holy city unto the Lord; wherefore, it could not be a new Jerusalem for it had been in a time of old; but it should be built up again, and become a holy city of the Lord; and it should be built unto the house of Israel—
>
> 6 And that a New Jerusalem should be built up upon this land, unto the remnant of the seed of Joseph, for which things there has been a type.
>
> 7 For as Joseph brought his father down into the land of Egypt, even so he died there; wherefore, the Lord brought a remnant of the seed of Joseph out of the land of Jerusalem, that he might be merciful unto the seed of Joseph that they should perish not, even as he was merciful unto the father of Joseph that he should perish not.
>
> 8 Wherefore, the remnant of the house of Joseph shall be built upon this land; and it shall be a land of their inheritance; and they shall build up a holy city unto the Lord, like unto the Jerusalem of old; and they shall no more be confounded, until the end come when the earth shall pass away.
>
> 9 And there shall be a new heaven and a new earth; and they shall be like unto the old save the old have passed away, and all things have become new.
>
> 10 And then cometh the New Jerusalem; and blessed are they who dwell therein, for it is they whose garments are white through the blood of the Lamb; and they are they who are numbered among the remnant of the seed of Joseph, who were of the house of Israel. (Ether 13:5–10)

God's Covenant with America

Jacob (the father of the twelve tribes of Israel) prophesied that part of his lineage, through Joseph, would make their way across the world to the bounds of the everlasting hills (see Genesis 49:26): a description that fits the great Rocky Mountains of North America, stretching across the land from the Pacific Northwest to New Mexico. We read this prophecy in the Bible:

> 22 Joseph is a fruitful bough, even a fruitful bough by a well; whose branches run over the wall.
>
> 23 The archers have sorely grieved him, and shot at him, and hated him:
>
> 24 But his bow abode in strength, and the arms of his hands were made strong by the hands of the mighty God of Jacob. . . .
>
> 26 The blessings of thy father have prevailed above the blessings of my progenitors unto the utmost bounds of the everlasting hills: they shall be on the head of Joseph, and on the crown of the head of him that was separate from his brethren. (Genesis 49:22–24, 26)

Genesis 49 points to America as a God-inspired nation: a nation whose history is picked up in the pages of the Book of Mormon (Mormon being a direct descendant of Lehi, who was a direct descendant of Joseph). Why America? Because it was destined that the restored gospel of Jesus Christ would roll forth among the nations (beginning in America) and would gather the scattered tribes of Israel in preparation for the Lord's triumphant return. Thus, America has been under the watchful eye of the Almighty right from the beginning. It was in America that the monarchial systems of the Old World were replaced with a constitutional government based on Judeo-Christian ideals. It was America that helped to successfully defeat the Communist dictatorships of Nazi Germany and Soviet Russia and other Middle Eastern tyrants, while leaving basic constitutional principles behind that have blessed those people and have prepared them to hear and embrace the gospel of Jesus Christ as it is introduced to them. The heavenly inspired Declaration of Independence and the Constitution have provided the people of America with certain inalienable rights (including life, liberty, and the pursuit of happiness), which have provided the fertile ground needed for Christianity to flourish in this land of promise: a land favored beyond any other nation on earth.

In George Washington's first inaugural address as the first president of the United States, it was apparent that Washington recognized God as the protector and ruler of this great nation. He said, "[I]t would be peculiarly improper to omit in this first official Act, my fervent supplications to that Almighty Being who rules over the Universe, . . . that his benediction may consecrate to the liberties and happiness of the people of the United States." Washington then warned, "We ought to be no less persuaded that the smiles of Heaven can never be expected on a nation that disregards the eternal rules of order and right, which Heaven itself has ordained."[1]

God has truly been at the helm in regards to America's rise to power among the nations. He is a God our people should not forget, or they will face the same fate as the Nephites and the Jaredites, who both turned their backs on God and were ultimately destroyed. The scriptures speak of the destruction of the wicked during our day as well. Yet few listen, thinking the world will endure forever in its current condition. Yet, be not deceived, for warnings have come down to those of our day, not only in the Bible, but also in the Book of Mormon and by prophets of the restored Church of Jesus Christ of Latter-day Saints. While standing in general conference, Elder Bruce R. McConkie said,

> I stand before the Church this day and raise the warning voice. It is a prophetic voice, for I shall say only what the apostles and prophets have spoken concerning our day. . . . It is a voice calling upon the Lord's people to prepare for the troubles and desolations which are about to be poured out upon the world without measure. For the moment we live in a day of peace and prosperity but it shall not ever be thus. Great trials lie ahead. All of the sorrows and perils of the past are but a foretaste of what is yet to be. [. . .] Bands of Gadianton robbers will infest every nation, immorality and murder and crime will increase, and it will seem as though every man's hand is against his brother.[2]

President Ezra Taft Benson reminds us that unless the wicked repent of their sinful ways, destruction is sure to come:

> The voice of warning is unto all people by the mouths of His servants. If this voice is not heeded, the angels of destruction will increasingly go forth, and the chastening hand of Almighty God will be felt upon the nations as decreed, until a full end thereof will be the result. Wars, devastation, and untold suffering will be your lot except you turn unto the Lord in humble repentance. Destruction, even more terrible and far-reaching than attended the last great war, will come with certainty unless rulers and people alike repent and cease their evil and godless ways. God will not be mocked. He will not permit the sins of sexual immorality, secret murderous combinations, the killing of the unborn, and disregard for all His holy commandments and the messages of

> His servants to go unheeded without grievous punishment for such wickedness. The nations of the world cannot endure in sin. The way of escape is clear. The immutable laws of God remain steadfastly in the heavens above. When men and nations refuse to abide by them, the penalty must follow. They will be wasted away. Sin demands punishment.[3]

The Church has continually admonished every righteous priesthood leader to sound the warning cry and to advise the Saints to prepare both physically and spiritually for the terrible times ahead. Noah warned the people of his day for 120 years. It has been over 120 years for us. Thus, we cannot expect the prophesied events destined to cleanse the land of the wicked to be held at bay much longer. In fact, they have already begun. So, it is more important than ever to be prepared, for there can be little doubt that the main part of the storm is quickly approaching. In truth, it is approaching much faster than any of us would like, with the need to prepare never emphasized more forcibly than it is today. In the following chapters, follow the history of the world from the days of Adam onward and see how the events of today have slowly unfolded; see how mankind has either risen in glory because of their righteousness, or fallen because of their sins. Then ask yourself: Where are we in regards to the prophesied signs of the coming of Christ?

Notes

1. George Washington's First Inaugural Address, quoted in Timothy Ballard, *The Covenant: One Nation Under God* (New York: Legends Library, 2012), 67.
2. Blaine and Brenton Yorgason, *Spiritual Survival in the Last Days* (Salt Lake City: Deseret Book, 1990), 49–50.
3. Ezra Taft Benson, *The Teachings of Ezra Taft Benson* (Salt Lake City: Bookcraft, 1988), 412–13.

1

In the Beginning

In the book of Genesis, we learn that our first parents, Adam and Eve, lived in a beautiful spot on the newly formed earth called the Garden of Eden. After disobeying God by partaking of the forbidden fruit, Adam and Eve were cast out of the garden and lived in a place called Adam-ondi-Ahman. In Doctrine and Covenants 116:1, we learn that Adam-ondi-Ahman was located in the northwest corner of Missouri. Life was not easy for Adam and Eve once they left the garden: Adam was now required to produce food by the sweat of his brow, and Eve was destined to bear children in pain and sorrow. Sadly, some of their children were not as righteous as their parents, and sin entered the land almost immediately when jealousies arose among siblings. Greed, pride, and avarice began to raise their ugly heads. The earliest story of such evils revolves around two of their sons Cain and Abel. Cain was jealous of his brother Abel, who walked in holiness before the Lord. While Abel brought of the firstlings of his flock as an offering to the Lord (an offering that was readily accepted by the Lord), Cain presented the fruit of the ground as an offering, which was rejected. The offering was in similitude of the Savior's blood sacrifice at the close of His mortal ministry. True to his benevolent nature, the Lord patiently tried to explain to Cain why his offering was unacceptable and warned Cain that Satan desired to have him. Rather than repent, Cain chose to be angry with God and refused to listen to Him any longer. Thus the Lord reluctantly delivered Cain up to Satan, saying "and it shall be unto thee according to his desire" (Moses 5:23).

Introduction of Secret Combinations

With Cain under Satan's influence, the stage was now set for Satan to introduce murder and mayhem into the world, in order to continue his efforts to destroy the family of God and any attempts they would make to attain salvation.

> 30 And Satan said unto Cain: Swear unto me by thy throat, and if thou tell it thou shalt die; and swear thy brethren by their heads, and by the living God, that they tell it not; for if they tell it, they shall surely die; and this that thy father may not know it; and this day I will deliver thy brother Abel into thine hands.
>
> 31 And Satan sware unto Cain that he would do according to his commands. And all these things were done in secret. (Moses 5:29–30)

Once the pact between Cain and Satan was made,

> 32 Cain went into the field, and Cain talked with Abel, his brother. And it came to pass that while they were in the field, Cain rose up against Abel, his brother, and slew him.
>
> 33 And Cain gloried in that which he had done, saying: I am free; surely the flocks of my brother falleth into my hands. (Moses 5:32–33).

Here we see the first seed planted for the establishment of the wicked idea of getting gain by any means, even murder. Cain was the first man on earth to feel the dangerous, exhilarating power of acquiring what did not belong to him, and he felt no regret about how he got it. He should have known that the Lord would have asked him to recount his actions, but when the Lord asked Cain where his brother was, he smugly said, "*I know not. Am I my brother's keeper*? (Moses 5:34; emphasis added). Knowing full well that Cain had killed his brother (thereby introducing murder into the world), the Lord cursed Cain with a sore cursing, saying,

> 37 A fugitive and a vagabond shalt thou be in the earth. . . .
>
> 41 And Cain was shut out from the presence of the Lord, and with his wife and many of his brethren dwelt in the land of Nod, on the east of Eden. (Moses 5:37, 41)

With Satan's evil influence now permeating their little colony, the children born to Cain and his wife became as wicked as their parents. One of the most important callings of humankind is to teach children about God and how to worship Him. Yet, it takes righteous parents to do so. The wicked take worldly things to be their gods, such as wealth, power, or glory. Thus, Cain's children followed in the footsteps of their wicked father, who the scriptures say, "*loved Satan more than God*" (Moses 5:18; emphasis added).

A Righteous Branch

Gratefully, not all the descendants of Adam and Eve followed after Satan. A righteous branch also existed (with Seth, who was born in the years following Abel's murder), and was preeminent among them. The early inhabitants of the earth lived extraordinarily long lives in those years, with the nine principle patriarchs between Adam and Noah being Seth, Enos, Cainan, Mahalaleel, Jared, Enoch, Methuselah, and Lamech (the father of Noah). During this span of time, the world filled with inhabitants, some good and some bad, with the bad quickly becoming the majority. And so, during the days of Enos (the son of Seth), the Lord instructed the righteous among them to separate from the wicked and dwell in a land of promise that He had named after his own son, Cainan[1] (see Moses 6:17). "Satan had great dominion among men, and raged in their hearts; and from thenceforth came wars and bloodshed; and a man's hand was against his own brother, in administering death, because of secret works, seeking for power" (Moses 6:15).

The Call to Repent

As things continued to go downhill, the Lord sent a famine upon the inhabitants of the earth, hoping to bring them to their knees in repentance, but to no avail. In fact, things continued to get worse. Nothing seemed to deter the wicked from their sinful ways. In Hugh Nibley's work on the apocryphal works related to Enoch, we learn that in time their wicked ways included incantations, drugs, astrology, and sorcery—all designed to teach men to emancipate themselves from God, not fully appreciating the fact that God rules the universe, not man.[2] The Lord said,

> 35 Behold, I am God; Man of Holiness is my name; Man of Counsel is my name; and Endless and Eternal is my name, also.
>
> 36 Wherefore, I can stretch forth mine hands and hold all the creations which I have made; and mine eye can pierce them also, and among all the workmanship of mine hands there has not been so great wickedness as among thy brethren. (Moses 7:35–36)

With such rampant wickedness sweeping across the pre-diluvium world, missionaries were needed to carry the voice of warning to the people. As is always the case, God turned to His patriarchs, who carried the priesthood from the days of Adam onward and had been faithful in crying repentance and baptism throughout their lives (see Moses 6:23). In this instance, he turned to Enoch, who proved to be one of the greatest missionaries of all time. Missionary work was desperately needed during Enoch's day, for while God had given man eyes to see and ears to hear and the power to understand God's commandments, "Satan had great dominion among men, and raged in their hearts; and from thenceforth came wars and bloodshed; and a man's hand was against his own brother" (Moses 6:15).

Enoch's Missionary Call and Mission

In one last effort to save His errant children, God sent Enoch on a mission. As Enoch journeyed along,

> 26 The Spirit of God descended out of heaven, and abode upon him.
>
> 27 And he heard a voice from heaven, saying: Enoch, my son, prophesy unto this people, and say unto them—Repent, for thus saith the Lord: I am angry with this people, and my fierce anger is kindled against them; for their hearts have waxed hard, and their ears are dull of hearing, and their eyes cannot see afar off;
>
> 28 And for these many generations, ever since the day that I created them, have they gone astray, and have denied me, and have sought their own counsels in the dark; and in their own abominations have they devised murder, and have not kept the commandments, which I gave unto their father, Adam.
>
> 29 Wherefore, they have foresworn themselves, and, by their oaths, they have brought upon themselves death; and a hell I have prepared for them, if they repent not. (Moses 6:26–29)

Enoch felt totally unprepared for such a mission, saying,

> 31 Why is it that I have found favor in thy sight, and am but a lad, and all the people hate me; for I am slow of speech; wherefore am I thy servant?
>
> 32 And the Lord said unto Enoch: Go forth and do as I have commanded thee, and no man shall pierce thee. Open thy mouth, and it shall be filled, and I will give thee utterance, for all flesh is in my hands, and I will do as seemeth me good. . . .
>
> 37 And it came to pass that Enoch went forth in the land, among the people, standing upon the hills and the high places, and cried with a loud voice, testifying against their works; and all men were offended because of him. (Moses 6:31–32, 37)

Enoch could not refrain from chastising the people, saying,

> 43 The Lord which spake with me, the same is the God of heaven, and he is my God, and your God, and ye are my brethren, and why counsel ye yourselves, and deny the God of Heaven? . . .
>
> 49 Behold Satan hath come among the children of men, and tempteth men to worship him; and men have become carnal, sensual, and devilish, and are shut out from the presence of God. (Moses 6:43, 49)

So powerful were the words of Enoch that the people trembled and could not even stand in his presence, for they all knew right from wrong. They also knew the principles of repentance and baptism because their fathers had been taught the plan of salvation from Adam himself, who learned from God, who taught Adam,

> 52 If thou wilt turn unto me, and hearken unto my voice, and believe, and repent of all thy transgressions, and be baptized, even in water, in the name of mine Only Begotten Son, who is full of grace and truth, which is Jesus Christ, the only name which shall be given under heaven, whereby salvation shall come unto the children of men, ye shall receive the gift of the Holy Ghost. . . .
>
> 60 For by the water ye keep the commandment; by the Spirit ye are justified, and by the blood ye are sanctified; . . .
>
> 62 And now, behold, I say unto you: This is the plan of salvation unto all men, through the blood of mine Only Begotten, who shall come in the meridian of time. (Moses 6:52, 60, 62)

Those who took the message of Enoch to heart rededicated themselves to the Lord and His work to bring about the salvation of man, while those who delighted in their wickedness rejected Enoch's message and ignored his call to repent.

The Call to Gather to Zion

Everywhere Enoch went he bore testimony of the Father and the Son. His message was either accepted or rejected, which divided men into two camps: the righteous and the wicked. Knowing that the righteous cannot live unspotted from the world while in the midst of the willfully wicked who continually try to debase or destroy the righteous, the Lord instilled the spirit of gathering in the righteous so that He might save them physically as well as spiritually.

> 17 The fear of the Lord was upon all nations, so great was the glory of the Lord, which was upon his people. And the Lord blessed the land, and they were blessed upon the mountains, and upon the high places, and did flourish.
>
> 18 And the Lord called his people Zion, because they were of one heart and one mind, and dwelt in righteousness; and there was no poor among them. (Moses 7:17–18).

The Zion of Enoch's day is a prototype of the Zion to come when the Lord will once again gather the righteous out from among the wicked, and protect them from the terrible upheavals of the latter days prior to the Savior's prophesied Second Coming.

Prophetic Visions of the Universal Flood

God revealed more and more of the mysteries of heaven to Enoch as time went by. The first thing Enoch was shown was the future of his own city. He was shown how it would eventually be removed from the earth and taken to a special place prepared for it, and he heard the Lord say, "*Behold mine abode forever*" (Moses 7:21; emphasis added). Enoch then saw the residue of the inhabitants of the earth (after he and his people were taken up and away from the earth), and that "the power of Satan was upon all the face of the earth" (Moses 7:24). The Lord said,

> 32 Behold these thy brethren; they are the workmanship of mine own hands, and I gave unto them their knowledge, in the day I created them; and in the Garden of Eden, gave I unto man his agency;
>
> 33 And unto thy brethren have I said, and also given commandment, that they should love one another, and that they should choose me,

their Father; but behold, they are without affection, and they hate their own blood;

34 And the fire of mine indignation is kindled against them; and in my hot displeasure will I send in the floods upon them, for my fierce anger is kindled against them. (Moses 7:32–34)

Enoch was understandably shaken by such a decree, and raised his hands toward heaven crying out in distress, pleading with the Lord for mankind. In answer to Enoch's heartfelt plea, God said, "*And the whole heavens shall weep over them, even all the workmanship of mine hands; wherefore should not the heavens weep, seeing these shall suffer?*" (Moses 7:37; emphasis added). The heavens no doubt weep for the lost part of our generation, as well as those who have forsaken God and gone astray. The prophesied Second Coming of Christ is at our very doors, and with it, another worldwide cleansing of the wicked.

Enoch Saw the Future of the World and the New Jerusalem

As more and more of the events leading up to the Flood of Noah's day were shown to Enoch, his sorrow grew until he could stand it no longer and could not be comforted. So, the Lord showed him the future of the world, even unto the coming of Jesus Christ in the meridian of time, and His ultimate Atonement for mankind.

47 And behold, Enoch saw the day of the coming of the Son of Man, even in the flesh; and his soul rejoiced, saying: The Righteous is lifted up, and the Lamb is slain from the foundation of the world; and through faith I am in the bosom of the Father, and behold, Zion is with me.

48 And it came to pass that Enoch looked upon the earth; and he heard a voice from the bowels thereof, saying: Wo, wo is me, the mother of men; I am pained, I am weary, because of the wickedness of my children. When shall I rest, and be cleansed from the filthiness which is gone forth out of me? When will my Creator sanctify me, that I may rest, and righteousness for a season abide upon my face?

49 And when Enoch heard the earth mourn, he wept, and cried unto the Lord, saying: O Lord, wilt thou not have compassion upon the earth? Wilt thou not bless the children of Noah? (Moses 7:47–49)

Enoch was ultimately given his answer:

> 61 And the day shall come that the earth shall rest, but before that day the heavens shall be darkened, and a veil of darkness shall cover the earth; and the heavens shall shake, and also the earth; and great tribulations shall be among the children of men, but my people will I preserve; . . .
>
> 62 And righteousness and truth will I cause to sweep the earth as with a flood, to gather out mine elect from the four quarters of the earth, unto a place which I shall prepare, an Holy City, that my people may gird up their loins, and be looking forth for the time of my coming; for there shall be my tabernacle, and it shall be called Zion, a New Jerusalem. . . .
>
> 64 And there shall be mine abode, and it shall be Zion, which shall come forth out of all the creations which I have made; and for the space of a thousand years the earth shall rest.
>
> 65 And it came to pass that Enoch saw the day of the coming of the Son of Man, in the last days, to dwell on the earth in righteousness for the space of a thousand years. (Moses 7:61–65)

The Translation of the City of Enoch

Enoch ruled his city in righteousness for 365 years before he and his beloved city of Zion were translated and removed from the earth to another place in the cosmos. The quickening of their bodies apparently neutralized the seeds of death, and they became subject to a higher physical law. A righteous branch of Enoch's posterity had to remain behind, however, to ensure that a righteous line would be perpetuated on through Noah. They were to provide missionaries to continue to preach repentance right up until the time of the cleansing flood. Their job was not an easy one, for Enoch beheld in vision that Satan "*had a great chain in his hand, and it veiled the whole face of the earth with darkness; and he looked up and laughed, and his angels rejoiced*" (Moses 7:26; emphasis added). Yet, the righteous who were converted during this last and final missionary call were caught up to Zion and away from Satan's power. Enoch even saw "angels descending out of heaven, bearing testimony of the Father and Son; and the Holy Ghost fell on [those who believed], and they *were caught up by the powers of heaven into Zion*" (Moses 7:27; emphasis added). Brigham Young commented that "He [Enoch] obtained power to translate himself and his people, with the region they inhabited, their houses, gardens, fields, cattle and all of their possessions."[3]

God's command to gather the righteous to Zion in Enoch's day is similar to the council given to the prophets of our day when the Lord declared:

> 7 Ye are called to bring to pass the gathering of mine elect; for mine elect hear my voice and harden not their hearts;
>
> 8 Wherefore the decree hath gone forth from the Father that they shall be gathered in unto one place upon the face of this land, to prepare their hearts and be prepared in all things against the day when tribulation and desolation are sent forth upon the wicked. (D&C 29:7–8)

Noah

Before Enoch and his city were caught up and away from the earth, he was privileged to see Noah (his progenitor) in a vision preaching repentance to the wicked of his day. Those who accepted Noah's call to repent were ultimately translated and taken up to dwell with the other righteous Saints in Enoch's city of Zion, while tragedy awaited those who rejected his call (see Moses 7:27).

The last step in the Lord's process of evacuation (that would last for generations) was to carry away the righteous of Noah's day unto Zion. But, missionary work continued right up to the end. Then, when all the preparations were made—the ark was finished, and the last of the righteous were caught up to Zion—the windows of heaven were opened. The fountains of the great deep were broken up and the rain began to fall. No one should have been surprised, however, for they had been warned for centuries. Thus, all that was left for the wicked who refused to repent was death.

The Universal Flood

Legends of the universal flood have been found in nearly every nation on earth. Many have been garbled into fanciful tales, such as those of Scandinavia.

> The stories of the Teutonic tribes of Scandinavia are vivid and describe terrifying events. The imagery of these legends emphasizes the size of the cataclysm. One such tale portrays the chaos of the world when the mighty wolf Fenrir shook himself and "made the whole world tremble.

> The aged ash tree Yggdrasil [envisaged as the axis of the earth] was shaken from its roots to its topmost branches. Mountains crumbled or split from top to bottom. . . ." Men "were driven from their hearths and the human race was swept from the surface of the earth. The earth itself was beginning to lose its shape. Already the stars were coming adrift from the sky and falling into the gaping void. . . . Flames spurted from fissures in the rocks; everywhere there was the hissing of steam. All living things, all plant life, were blotted out. . . . And now all the rivers, all the seas rose and overflowed. From every side waves lashed against waves. They swelled and boiled and slowly covered all things. The earth sank beneath the sea. . . ." Then slowly "the earth emerged from the waves. Mountains rose anew. . . . Men also reappeared. . . . Enclosed in the wood itself of the ash tree Yggdrasil . . . the ancestors of a future race of men had escaped death."[4]

As fascinating as legends of the universal flood are, none are more informative than the episode provided in the Bible, which reads,

> 6 And Noah *was* six hundred years old when the flood of waters was upon the earth.
>
> 7 And Noah went in, and his sons, and his wife, and his sons' wives with him, into the ark, because of the waters of the flood.
>
> 8 Of clean beasts, and of beasts that *are* not clean, and of fowls, and of every thing that creepeth upon the earth, . . .
>
> 10 And it came to pass after seven days, that the waters of the flood were upon the earth.
>
> 11 In the six hundredth year of Noah's life, in the second month, the seventeenth day of the month, the same day were all the fountains of the great deep broken up, and the windows of heaven were opened. . . .
>
> 19 And the waters prevailed exceedingly upon the earth; and all the high hills, that *were* under the whole heaven, were covered. . . .
>
> 21 And all flesh died that moved upon the earth, both of fowl, and of cattle, and of beast, and of every creeping thing that creepeth upon the earth, and every man. . . .
>
> 23 Noah only remained *alive,* and they that *were* with him in the ark.
>
> 24 And the waters prevailed upon the earth an hundred and fifty days. (Genesis 7:6–8, 10–11, 19, 21, 23–24; emphasis added)

As we move on through the centuries of history that followed the great flood of Noah's day, we will see that the Lord used the same pattern over and over again among the growing nations of the world. Prophecies of impending doom always precede the destruction of the wicked. And so it is in our day. Just as it was in the days of Enoch, missionaries are continuously scouring the earth in search of the honest in heart who will learn of Christ's fulfillment of His mission as the Savior of the world during the meridian of time. He did so through His infinite Atonement at the end of His mortal ministry. The Atonement is a gift, which upon repentance, can release the penitent from their sins and save them from the destruction destined to fall upon the wicked. Thus, there is hope for all in Christ.

Notes

1. *Book of Jasher* 1:33. Cainan was named after the son of Enos, and in no way relates to Cain, whose people settled in the land of Cainaan; note the different spelling of the name.
2. Hugh Nibley, *Enoch the Prophet* (Salt Lake City: Deseret Book, 1986), 17.
3. Brigham Young quoted in W. Cleon Skousen, *The First 2000 Years* (Salt Lake City: Bookcraft, 1953), 191–92.
4. "Flood," Rebecca Conoly and Russell Grigg, *Creation.com*, October 12, 2011, creation.com/many-flood-legends#txtRef9. See also Felix Guirand, *The Larousse Encyclopedia of Mythology* (London: Chancellor Press, 1996), 275–77.

2

The Jaredites

Once the floodwaters abated, Noah, his family, and all the animals they brought with them left the ark and went their separate ways. "God blessed Noah and his sons, and said unto them, *Be fruitful, and multiply, and replenish the earth*" (Genesis 9:1; emphasis added). Noah's sons kept that commandment, for they and their wives began to procreate immediately. As children were born during their long lives, the population of the world grew. The family of Japheth (who had seven sons) grew to four hundred and sixty men. The five sons of Shem increased in numbers to three hundred men. The four sons of Ham grew to seven hundred and thirty men, one of which was Nimrod, who became a mighty man and was highly esteemed.[1]

Nimrod's False Religion

As Nimrod continued to grow in power, he built a great city in a valley he named Shinar. Hearing of his fame and the grandeur of his city, people came from every direction to bow down before him and to acknowledge him as their lord and king, not caring that he was a wicked man who had forgotten the ways of the Lord.

> And all the earth was of one tongue and words of union, but Nimrod did not go in the ways of the Lord, and he was more wicked than all the men that were before him, from the days of the flood until those days.
>
> And they made gods of wood and stone, and he bowed down to them, and he rebelled against the Lord, and taught all his subjects and the people of the earth his wicked ways.[2]

Under Satan's influence, Nimrod and the post-flood populations turned to other forms of religion, leaving behind the true worship of God. Sun worship ultimately became one of the most dominant. We learn from the Pearl of Great Price that the people of Abraham's day (a contemporary of Nimrod), went after strange gods, such as "the god of Elkenah, and the god of Libnah, and the god of Mahmackrah, and the god of Korash, and the god of Pharaoh, king of Egypt" (Abraham 1:6), and the god of Shagreel, who was the sun (see Abraham 1:9).

The Tower of Babel

As time passed, the princes of Nimrod counseled together and decided to build a great city with a tower high enough to reach to heaven. Unfortunately, the construction of the tower had sinister overtones, for its lofty top was intended to provide them with a place for sacrifice and worship—not to worship Jehovah, but to worship the gods the devil had introduced to them. The tower of Babel must have been a magnificent sight, yet one not destined to outlast its time, for God knew the wicked intent of the hearts of the builders of the tower. God stood before the angels that were with Him and said,

> 7 Go to, let us go down, and there confound their language, that they may not understand one another's speech.
>
> 8 So the Lord scattered them abroad from thence upon the face of all the earth: and they left off to build the city.
>
> 9 Therefore is the name of it called Babel; because the Lord did there confound the language of all the earth: and from thence did the Lord scatter them abroad upon the face of all the earth. (Genesis 11:7–9)

The Jaredites

To preserve the few remaining righteous people from such growing corruption, the Lord led Jared, his brother, their families, and their friends halfway across the world to a land choice above all other lands—a land of promise. After much preparation, and a harrowing journey across the great deep, Ether 6:12 informs us "they did land upon the shore of the promised land."

The New Jerusalem

One of the most defining features of the promised land is the Lord's declaration that the New Jerusalem would rise in that favored land. Moroni said:

> 2 After the waters had receded from off the face of this land it became a choice land above all other lands, a chosen land of the Lord; wherefore the Lord would have that all men should serve him who dwell upon the face thereof;
>
> 3 And that it was the place of the New Jerusalem, which should come down out of heaven, and the holy sanctuary of the Lord. (Ether 13:2–3)

The Nephites were also told of the sacred nature of the land and the rise of the New Jerusalem. After Christ's death and Resurrection, when the risen Lord was speaking to the multitude of Nephites in Bountiful, He spoke about the future of the promised land, saying: "And behold, this people will I establish in this land, unto the fulfilling of the covenant which I made with your father Jacob; and it shall be a New Jerusalem. And the powers of heaven shall be in the midst of this people; yea, even I will be in the midst of you" (3 Nephi 20:22).

In a revelation to our modern prophets, the Lord declared exactly where that holy city would be built.

> 1 Hearken, O ye elders of my church, saith the Lord your God, who have assembled yourselves together, according to my commandments, in this land, which is the land of Missouri, which is the land which I have appointed and consecrated for the gathering of the saints.
>
> 2 Wherefore, this is the land of promise, and the place for the city of Zion. (D&C 57:1–2)

Now, if the New Jerusalem is to be built in *this land* (as prophesied in Ether 13:8), and we know by modern revelation that the New Jerusalem is to be built in the western borders of Missouri (see D&C 84:3), then this promised land must be America. Like the people of Enoch's day, the Jaredites fully understood their responsibility in keeping the holy land of America clean of corruption, for they were told in no uncertain terms that it was an everlasting decree by God that only those nations who lived in the land righteously would prosper: "For behold, this is a land which is choice above all other lands; wherefore he that doth possess it shall serve God or shall be swept off; for it is the everlasting decree of

God. And it is not until the fulness of iniquity among the children of the land, that they are swept off" (Ether 2:10).

The Jaredites' Geographic Location

From all the evidence available, the geographic homeland of the Nephites appears to have been in the regions around New York's Hill Cumorah, with outlying posts in various regions throughout the great northeastern woodlands. The land was just as the Lord said it would be—"a land choice above all others" (Ether 2:15). It had lush forests, sweeping meadows, and numerous lakes and wetlands where geese, ducks, and swans stopped on their migratory routes back and forth across the country. By examining fossil samples and the radiocarbon dates pertinent to this region, it was determined that the northeast experienced a warm, moist climate following the Ice Age, which considerably surpassed the present in average warmth. Such conditions accelerated the melting of the great glaciers, which left behind numerous large bodies of waters, as well as ponds, rivers, and streams. The northeastern woodlands have the added advantage of having a fairly consistent rainfall. Moreover, the woodlands are graced by the five magnificent Great Lakes that stretch a thousand miles across the land—the combined lakes constituting the greatest freshwater system on earth. This was truly "a land choice above all others"; a land the Jaredites would call home for the next millennium and a half.

The Book of Mormon places the Jaredites' land of first inheritance somewhere to the west of the Hill Cumorah (also called the hill Ramah, see Ether 15:11). The relics left behind by those who lived in the area during Jaredite times are the most heavily concentrated in western New York, between the Niagara and Genesee rivers. Archaeological evidence shows that, in time, the early occupants of western New York came to settle by trade and conquest lands scattered from the Atlantic to the Mississippi. Those in each separate region were given a different cultural name—a subject far too lengthy for this body of work. A much more detailed account of the lands they settled can be found in *The Lost Sheep of Ancient America: Bringing the Lands and People of the Book of Mormon to Life.*[3]

Fulness of Iniquity

Sadly, all too many of the Jaredites proved to be wicked almost from the beginning. Once the majority of the Jaredites became wicked, the Lord cursed the land with a sore cursing in hopes of bringing them to repentance (just as he had done to those in the days prior to the terrible flood of Noah's day). Unfortunately, just as it was in the days prior to the flood, nothing seemed to deter the Jaredites from their wicked ways. Plague after plague and draught after draught followed, causing famine on an unprecedented scale, yet nothing brought the people to their knees in repentance.

Wickedness Ultimately Brings Destruction

Sadly, during the reign of the Jaredite king Omer, the secret works of darkness were once again discovered and embraced by the people. King Omer's own son hoped to use them to dethrone his father and claim the crown for himself. The devil had been using these secret works of darkness to corrupt the world ever since he introduced them to Cain. In his efforts to bring down the post-diluvium world, the devil fully intended to set his powers into motion again; this time the Jaredites proved to be willing subjects.

Helaman recognized the evil one as the author of such secret works during Nephite times when he said, "And also it is that same being who put it into the hearts of the people to build a tower sufficiently high that they might get to heaven. And it was that same being who led on the people who came from that tower into this land; who spread the works of darkness and abominations over all the face of the land, until he dragged the people down to an entire destruction, and to an everlasting hell" (Helaman 6:28).

True to form, the Lord warned righteous King Omer to take his family and flee before He took vengeance upon the wicked. Omer was told to flee to a place called Ablom—a place just to the east of the Hill Cumorah. They stayed there until the Lord told them it was safe to return. "And the Lord warned Omer in a dream that he should depart out of the land; wherefore Omer departed out of the land with his family, and traveled many days, and came over and passed by the hill of Shim, and came over by the place where the Nephites were destroyed, and from thence eastward, and came to a place which was called Ablom, by the seashore, and there he pitched his tent, and also his sons and his daughters, and all his household, save it were Jared and his family" (Ether 9:3).

The above scripture makes it clear that King Omer and those who were with him traveled eastward from their western New York homeland to a place of safety a little beyond the Hill Cumorah (the place where the Nephites were destroyed). They settled near a seashore, which in this setting could be the north end of one of the Finger Lakes (to the east of Cumorah) or the great Montezuma Marsh—all of which were greater in size than they are today.

The End Finally Comes

As the sad tale of the Jaredites continued, we find Omer safely settled in Ablom, and his son Jared sat on his father's throne. While Jared's ambition to dethrone his father was successful, the kingdom would not know peace under his short rule. His new son-in-law, Akish, had now set his own sights on the kingdom, and with nothing but warfare following, they fought for years. Battle after battle raged across the land. Ultimately resulting in the near extinction of the entire kingdom. All but thirty souls and the household of Omer were killed. This was no small event in the history of the Jaredites. Yet, as tragic as the war was, the kingdom was not destined for complete extinction—at least not yet. As is always the case, the Lord continued to warn them through the voice of His prophets and the elements themselves to repent or be destroyed.

Unfortunately, no matter how many disasters the Lord sent upon the wicked to bring them to their knees in repentance, they continued in their sinful ways. Thus, the Lord had the prophet Ether warn them one last time, saying that if they did not repent, He would not send disease and famines upon them this time, but would wipe them off the face of the earth. Ether tried to explain to the people that this was "a land choice above all others" (Ether 2:15), and this was the place where the Lord would rule the nations from the New Jerusalem for a thousand years of peace, but they refused to listen. The wickedness of the people was so deeply ingrained in them that they ignored his prophetic warnings. In consequence, he began to record the history of his people. This would not be an easy task, however, because warfare raged all across the land. Ether had been cast out and forced to hide in the cavity of a rock to make his recording, while viewing the awful scenes of destruction around him.

The scriptures explain that the Jaredites' final battles took them eastward from the land of their first inheritance. "It came to pass that Shiz did pursue Coriantumr *eastward*" (Ether 14:26; emphasis added). Continuing east and north would have led them to the great waters of Ripliancum—no doubt Lake Ontario, for the scriptures explain that Ripliancum means "large, or to exceed all" (Ether 15:8)—a body of water much larger in size than their local seas. From Ripliancum, they then moved south to the Hill Cumorah (or Ramah), the only known landmark we have of that ancient time in history.

The Battle Scene at Ramah

In speaking of the Hill Cumorah, the Hill Ramah, and the waters of Ripliancum, Joseph Fielding Smith said,

> It is known that the *Hill Cumorah* where the Nephites were destroyed is the hill where the Jaredites were also destroyed. This hill was known to the Jaredites as *Ramah*. It was approximately near the waters of Ripliancum, which the Book of Ether says, "by interpretation is large, or to exceed all." Mormon adds: "And it came to pass that we did march forth to the land of Cumorah, and we did pitch our tents round about the hill Cumorah; and it was in a land of many waters, rivers, and fountains; and here we had hope to gain advantage over the Lamanites."
>
> It must be conceded that this description fits perfectly the land of Cumorah in New York, as it has been known since the visitation of Moroni to the Prophet Joseph Smith, for the hill is in the proximity of the Great Lakes and also in the land of many rivers and fountains. Moreover, the Prophet Joseph Smith himself is on record, definitely declaring the present hill called Cumorah to be the exact hill spoken of in the Book of Mormon.[4]

As was the custom of the Jaredite times, a period of four years was agreed upon so the final armies could gather together their people from all the outlying regions for one final showdown. When the allotted time had passed, and the Jaredites had gathered together their people (even their women and little children) in two bodies—all armed with breast-plates, head-plates, and all manner of weapons of war—they marched forth to battle (see Ether 15:15). Nothing can adequately describe the horror of the scene when the battle ended. Thus, let the scriptures speak for themselves:

> 15 They fought all that day, and conquered not.
>
> 16 And it came to pass that when it was night they were weary, and retired to their camps; and after they had retired to their camps they took up a howling and a lamentation for the loss of the slain of their people; and so great were their cries, their howlings and lamentations, that they did rend the air exceedingly.
>
> 17 And it came to pass that on the morrow they did go again to battle, and great and terrible was that day; nevertheless, they conquered not, and when the night came again they did rend the air with their cries, and their howlings, and their mournings, for the loss of the slain of their people. (Ether 15:15–17)

In spite of such terrible losses, the battle raged on the next day and then the next, and on and on until only two men, Shiz and Coriantumr, remained alive out of all their people, all save Ether who was hiding away, recording the horror of the war and the final extermination of his people. In a long, protracted struggle between the two men, Coriantumr came out the victor, only to roam the land as a lonely and broken man until discovered by the Mulekites sometime later (see Omni 1:20–21).

A Latter-day Saint View of Events

Marion G. Romney said,

> In the western part of the state of New York near Palmyra is a prominent hill known as the "hill Cumorah." (Mormon 6:6). On July twenty-fifth of this year, as I stood on the crest of that hill admiring with awe the breathtaking panorama which stretched out before me on every hand, my mind reverted to the events which occurred in that vicinity some twenty-five centuries ago—events which brought to an end the great Jaredite nation. . . .
>
> As I contemplated this tragic scene from the crest of Cumorah and viewed the beautiful land of the Restoration as it appears today, I cried in my soul, "How could it have happened? . . .
>
> The answer came immediately as I remembered that some fifteen to twenty centuries before their destruction, as the small group of their ancestors was being divinely led from the tower of Babel, the Lord "would that they should come forth even unto [this] land of promise,

> which was choice above all other lands, which the Lord God had preserved for a righteous people."
>
> And he had sworn in his wrath unto the brother of Jared [their prophet-leader], that whoso should possess this land . . . from that time henceforth and forever, should serve him, the true and only God, or they should be swept off when the fulness of his wrath should come upon them. . . .
>
> The tragic fate of the Jaredite and Nephite civilizations is proof positive that the Lord meant it when he said that this "is a land of promise; and whatsoever nation shall possess it shall serve God, or they shall be swept off when the fulness of his wrath shall come upon them. And the fulness of his wrath cometh upon the when they are ripened in iniquity. (Ether 2:9)[5]

In contemplating the events of that terrible time in history, Oliver Cowdery, who once stood gazing upon the Hill Cumorah where the final battle between the Jaredites took place, recited his own impression of that tragic affair.

> This hill, by the Jaredites, was called Ramah: by it, or around it pitched the famous army of Coriantumr their tents. Coriantumr was the last king of the Jaredites. The opposing army were to the west, and in this same vally *[sic]*, and near by, from day to day, did that mighty race spill their blood, in wrath, contending, as it were, brother against brother, and father, against son. In this same spot, in full view from the top of this same hill, one may gaze with astonishment upon the ground which was twice covered with the dead and dying of our fellow men. Here may be seen where once sunk to nought the pride and strength of two mighty nations; and here . . . may be contemplated, in solitude, while nothing but the faithful record of Mormon and Moroni is now extant to inform us of the fact, scenes of misery and distress—the aged, whose silver locks in other places and at other times would command reverence; the mother, who in other circumstances would be spared from violence; the infant, whose tender cries would be regarded and listened to with a feeling of compassion and tenderness; and the virgin, whose grace, beauty and modesty, would be esteemed and held inviolate by all good men and enlightened and civilized nations, alike disregarded and treated with scorn!—in vain did the hoary head and man of gray hairs ask for mercy; in vain did the mother plead for compassion; in vain did the helpless and harmless infant weep for verry *[sic]* anguish, and in vain did the virgin seek to escape the ruthless hand of revengeful foes and demons in human form—all alike were trampled down by

> the feet of the strong, and crushed beneath the rage of battle and war! Alas, who can reflect upon the last struggle of great and populous nations, sinking to dust beneath (the hand of Justice and retribution without) weeping over the corruptions of the human heart, and sighing for the hour when the clangor of arms shall no more be heard, nor the calamities of contending armies no more experienced for a thousand years? Alas, the calamity of war, the extinction of nations, the ruin of kingdoms, the fall of empires, and the dissolution of governments! O the misery, distress and evil attendant on these![6]

In spite of the bounties the Lord offered the Jaredites, they ultimately forgot the Lord and His everlasting decree that only those nations that worshipped Him would prosper in the promised land, and that all others would be wiped away once they became ripe in iniquity. Without question, the wickedness of the Jaredites was full to overflowing—a decree which cannot be stated too often, for today we are faced with the same issue. Will we of this dispensation repent and obey the laws of God, or will we also ripen in iniquity until, like the Jaredites, we are totally destroyed?

> 35 The hour is not yet, but is nigh at hand, when peace shall be taken from the earth, and the devil shall have power over his own dominion.
>
> 36 And also the Lord shall have power over his saints, and shall reign in their midst, and shall come down in judgment upon . . . the world. (D&C 1:35–36)

Here we are again reminded of the prophesied coming of Christ who will once and for all purge the world of its wickedness, and will rule as rightful king over the pure in heart for a thousand years of blessed peace.

Notes

1. *Book of Jasher* (Salt Lake City: J. H. Parry & Company, 2007), 14.
2. Ibid., 16.
3. Phyllis Carol Olive, *The Lost Sheep of Ancient America: Bringing the Lands and People of the Book of Mormon to Life* (Springville, UT: Cedar Fort, Inc., 2015).
4. Joseph Fielding Smith, *Doctrines of Salvation*, comp. Bruce R. McConkie (Salt Lake City: Bookcraft, 1992), 3:233–34; italics in original.
5. Marion G. Romney, "America's Destiny, *Ensign*, November 1975.
6. Dean C. Jessee, ed., *The Papers of Joseph Smith* (Salt Lake City: Deseret Book, 2008), 1:79–80.

3

The Arrival of the Nephites

The saga played out in the Book of Mormon is simply a continuation of the saga played out in the Bible. Shem, one of Noah's three sons, was given the patriarchal birthright, which was passed down through the ages to Abraham, the grandfather of Jacob. Jacob's twelve sons became the twelve tribes of Israel (Jacob's name was changed to Israel by the Lord). While most of Jacob's sons remained in the Old World, the line of Joseph broke away from the other tribes and was led by the hand of the Lord to America, where they founded a new nation. In 3 Nephi, the Lord acknowledges the Nephites as a branch of His covenant people. During His visit to America (after His death and Resurrection), the Lord said, "Ye are the children of the prophets; and ye are of the house of Israel; and ye are of the covenant which the Father made with your fathers" (3 Nephi 20:25).

Lands as Inheritances

Specific lands were set aside as an inheritance for the twelve tribes of Israel, with Joseph's seed being given America as an everlasting inheritance. The prophet Lehi, the great progenitor of the Nephite nation, said the following after arriving in the promised land, "Notwithstanding our afflictions, we have obtained a land of promise, a land which is choice above all other lands; a land which the Lord God hath covenanted with me should be a land for the inheritance of my seed. Yea, the Lord hath covenanted this land unto me, and to my children forever, and also all those who should be led out of other countries by the hand of the Lord [meaning the Gentiles of the latter days]" (2 Nephi 1:5).

How It All Began

Because Jacob's sons and their descendants, which now constituted the twelve tribes of Israel, began to worship their neighbor's pagan gods rather than Jehovah (the one who rescued their fathers from Egyptian captivity and ultimately led them to what today is Israel), the Lord marked the city of Jerusalem for destruction. As things in Jerusalem continued to go downhill and its fall seemed imminent, a number of prophets, including Lehi, began to prophesy about the destruction of Jerusalem that would occur if the people did not repent. Lehi loved his people and his homeland and could not bear the thought of their destruction. Thus, he knelt and prayed to the Lord with all his heart on behalf of his countrymen: "And it came to pass as he prayed unto the Lord, there came a pillar of fire and dwelt upon a rock before him; and he saw and heard much; and because of the things which he saw and heard he did quake and tremble exceedingly" (1 Nephi 1:6).

Nephi Also Proves to Be a Prophet

In his desire to understand the visions his father had seen, Nephi also went to the Lord in prayer and was blessed with profound visions of his own.

> 1 For it came to pass after I had desired to know the things that my father had seen, and believing that the Lord was able to make them known unto me, as I sat pondering in mine heart I was caught away in the Spirit of the Lord, yea, into an exceedingly high mountain, which I never had before seen, and upon which I never had before set my foot.
>
> 2 And the Spirit said unto me: Behold, what desirest thou?
>
> 3 And I said: I desire to behold the things which my father saw. (1 Nephi 11:1–3)

During Nephi's visionary experience, he was not only given the interpretation of his father's vision, but also a vision of his own, which included a vision of Mary holding her holy child, and a vision of the Messiah's mortal ministry. He was also shown the land of promise and was told that the risen Lord would one day visit His people in the promised land, but that their future after His visit depended upon either their righteousness or iniquity. For if they turned to iniquity after having been so blessed as to see the Savior, they would be doomed to destruction.

Lehi Is Warned to Depart Jerusalem

After learning of the fate of Jerusalem, Lehi valiantly went out among his countrymen to prophesy and implore them to return to the ways of the Lord, lest their city be destroyed. Rather than repent, however, they mocked him, cast stones at him, and sought to take away his life. Nephi later recounts that the Lord spoke to Lehi in a dream and said,

> 1 Blessed art thou Lehi, because of the things which thou hast done; and because thou hast been faithful and declared unto this people the things which I commanded thee, behold, they seek to take away thy life.
>
> 2 And it came to pass that the Lord commanded my father, even in a dream, that he should take his family and depart into the wilderness. (1 Nephi 2:1–2)

Not surprisingly, Lehi quickly gathered up his family of daughters and four sons, and, through a series of return visits to Jerusalem, the family of Ishmael and the servant of Laban, and made haste out of the city. With not-so-friendly nations in control of the Mediterranean ports, the Lord had Lehi's company detour into the Arabian Desert where they spent eight years in the wilderness being tempered, strengthened, and prepared for their long journey across the great deep. After those eight years in the wilderness, Nephi was instructed by the Lord to build a ship that would carry them across the sea to the promised land (see 1 Nephi 18:1–3).

Once the ship Nephi built was finished, they set off into the vast and boundless sea where they were carried by various currents around the southern tip of Africa and into the Atlantic Ocean. From there, the winds and currents would have carried them north up the west coast of Africa. After some three thousand miles, the currents then hook westward to South America where Nephi and his family would have found the North Equatorial Current and then the Gulf Stream. These currents would have carried them north all the way to Chesapeake Bay, where they could have sailed inland along the Susquehanna River—one of the oldest rivers in the world.

Somewhere along its shores, Joseph Smith Jr. and Oliver Cowdery later received the Melchizedek priesthood from the hands of Peter, James, and John (see D&C 128:20). Little did the early Saints of Joseph's day know that those living in New York and Pennsylvania were living right in the heart of Book of Mormon territory.

The Lands of Their First Inheritance

By following the Susquehanna River inland, the Nephites would have found themselves near the Susquehannock State Forest, where game was plentiful. The area between Lake Erie and the Susquehannock State Forest is filled with dozens of vineyards today. This region was perfectly suited for the Nephites who were commanded to keep the law of Moses, and wine was essential to their religious worship. The Lord purposely led them to a region that had four distinct seasons, so they could comply with all of the ordinances of the law of Moses. The rich alluvial bottomlands were favorable for cultivation, and produced rich yields of a variety of fruits and foodstuffs. The entire region was capable of supporting a numerous and industrious population.

> 23 And it came to pass that after we had sailed for the space of many days we did arrive at the promised land; and we went forth upon the land, and did pitch our tents; and we did call it the promised land.
>
> 24 And it came to pass that we did begin to till the earth, and we began to plant seeds; yea, we did put all our seeds into the earth, which we had brought from the land of Jerusalem. And it came to pass that they did grow exceedingly; wherefore, we were blessed in abundance. (1 Nephi 18:23–24)

As time passed, Nephi continued to prove to be a righteous man, as was his brother Jacob, both providing some of the most profound doctrine and spiritual insights found in any recorded scripture. But their brothers, Laman and Lemuel, were not so noble. In fact, they continually sought to destroy Nephi for the perceived sin of usurping the power of leadership that they, as the older brothers, felt rightly belonged to them. With Satan urging the older brothers and their people on, nothing the Nephites could do appeased them. Thus, the Lord warned Nephi to take his young family, and any who would follow him, and seek a new settlement Thus, they continued northward into southwestern New York, where they settled an area that they called the land of Nephi.

New York, a Great Natural Empire

The state of New York appears to have always been destined to be a great natural empire. Its geographic position, physical features, and abundance of natural resources have always made it a favorable place to settle. It also has a variety of soils capable of nourishing numerous types of vegetation, particularly food plants. Even today, the great valleys and alluvial plains are covered by heavy, easily cultivated deposits of fertile soil that is capable of sustaining immense fields of vegetables and grains. More than five thousand square miles in western New York and parts of neighboring Pennsylvania are still considered one vast farmland. Much of the superiority of the region is due to its local lakes and river systems that are fed by a vast number of secondary tributaries, many of which are navigable almost to their heads. Of almost equal importance are the natural overland trails that follow the shorelines of the ancient lakes that once filled so much of the land and the local forests abounding with wildlife. Thus there can be little doubt that the Lord led the Nephites to "a land choice above all others" (see Ether 2:15). It is a region highly desirable even today.

The Nephites Settle In

Once the Nephites settled a favorable location, they gave thanks and rejoiced in the bounteous blessings that the Lord had poured down on them. But, all in all (at least in the first few centuries), the Nephites proved to be a righteous people, worthy of the blessings of the Lord. Their understanding of Jesus Christ and His work among humankind was known to them from the very beginning. Nephi expounded upon Christ's mission as the Holy One of Israel as early as 550 BC,

> 23 For we labor diligently to write, to persuade our children, and also our brethren, to believe in Christ, and to be reconciled to God; for we know that it is by grace that we are saved, after all we can do. . . .
>
> 26 And we talk of Christ, we rejoice in Christ, we preach of Christ, we prophesy of Christ, and we write according to our prophecies, that our children may know to what source they may look for a remission of their sins. . . .
>
> 29 And now behold, I say unto you that the right way is to believe in Christ, and deny him not; and Christ is the Holy One of Israel; wherefore ye must bow down before him, and worship him with all

> your might, mind, and strength, and your whole soul; and if ye do this ye shall in nowise be cast out. (2 Nephi 25:23, 26, 29)

From Out of the Dust

The archaeological record speaks of ancient newcomers to the land between 600 BC and AD 400, which we can take to be the Nephite and Mulekite populations. During that long span of time, these two cultures established what archaeologists refer to as the Point Peninsula culture, named after an island at the east end of Lake Ontario where some of their artifacts were found. Those who settled in lower Ontario, however, have subsequently come to be known as the Saugeen culture, after the Saugeen River. The Proto-Algonquian language could be traced to the Saugeen and Point Peninsula people living in southern Ontario by Niagara Falls[1]—around 2,500 to 3,000 years ago—near the time the Mulekites settled Zarahemla, an area to the southeast of Niagara, along the north shores of Lake Erie, in what is today Buffalo, New York. The Mulekites held the lands to the north of the Nephites in their possession for nearly five centuries before the Nephites living in southwestern New York finally joined them in Zarahemla, just off the coast of Lake Erie sometime between 279 BC and 130 BC. Their expansion north around this time is also the same time archaeologists show an expansion of Point Peninsula ceramics from New York northeastward toward the Maritime Provinces along the Atlantic coast. Like the Jaredites before them, the Nephites filled up more of the land than the limited region that made up their spiritual heartland in Zarahemla.

New York State archaeologist William A. Richie revealed what a wide area of distribution the merged Point Peninsula culture ultimately settled:

> The western limits of the range probably reach into southern Manitoba and certainly include northern Minnesota. On the east, the culture can be traced across northern Maine and New Hampshire into New Brunswick. These peripheral limits are vaguely defined, and almost entirely on the basis of ceramic remains, and the same is true on the southern marches, which include southern New York and New England, and to the north beyond the Height of Land separating the drainage of the Great Lakes and St. Lawrence River from that of Hudson Bay.[2]

While their overall area of occupation is very widespread, Ritchie maintains that the cultural heartland of the Point Peninsula people appears to lie in the restricted regions between Lake Huron and Georgian Bay (to the west of Niagara Falls, with the Ottawa River to the north, the Richelieu River and Lake Champlain to the east, and the north shore of Lake Erie across the and the Seneca River to the south[3])—the very place we find the Hill Cumorah. While the New York setting may seem small to some, every geographic landmark mentioned in the Book of Mormon can be reconciled with that area (particularly western New York, between Lake Erie and the Genesee River Valley). Even its size can be reconciled. We might remember that Bountiful was described as being only one-and-a-half day's journey wide. When King Mosiah called the people forth to hear the account of Zeniff, he called forth *all* of the people, which by this time included not only the Nephites but the Mulekites as well. It was an enormous group, but one still small enough to be taught (albeit in two separate groups). Moreover, those who were baptized following that sobering occasion continued their instructions in the various churches scattered throughout the land (the number of which was only *seven*), far fewer than one would expect for the entire Northeastern Woodlands (see Mosiah 25:18–24). Surely this was a limited region, but one of the most desirable in the entire Northeast.

Nephite Prophecy

Throughout the years, Nephite prophets continued to preach of Christ in the various churches across the land. They taught of His mission among the scattered tribes of Israel, and even of His coming appearance to their very own people following His death and Resurrection—a time preceded by terrible upheavals of nature. Nephi began prophesying about this distant time in their people's future centuries prior to the time the events would actually take place. This gave the Nephites ample time to continually check and recheck their behavior, lest they ultimately be destroyed. Nephi said:

> 3 And after the Messiah shall come there shall be signs given unto my people of his birth, and also of his death and resurrection; and great and terrible shall that day be unto the wicked, for they shall perish; and they perish because they cast out the prophets, and the saints, and stone them, and slay them; wherefore the cry of the blood of the saints shall ascend up to God from the ground against them.

> 6 And they shall be visited with thunderings, and lightnings, and earthquakes, and all manner of destructions, for the fire of the anger of the Lord shall be kindled against them, and they shall be as stubble, and the day that cometh shall consume them, saith the Lord of Hosts.
>
> 7 O the pain, and the anguish of my soul for the loss of the slain of my people! For I, Nephi, have seen it, and it well nigh consumeth me before the presence of the Lord; but I must cry unto my God: Thy ways are just.
>
> 8 But behold, the righteous that hearken unto the words of the prophets, and destroy them not, but look forward unto Christ with steadfastness for the signs which are given, notwithstanding all persecution—behold, they are they which shall not perish.
>
> 9 But the Son of Righteousness shall appear unto them; and he shall heal them, and they shall have peace with him, until three generations shall have passed away, and many of the fourth generation shall have passed away in righteousness. (2 Nephi 26:3, 6–9)

Nephi even prophesied of the future destruction of his own people, which would occur after they abandoned the ways of the Lord and became a wicked people. This foreknowledge left Nephi bowed down with grief.

> 10 And when these things have passed away a speedy destruction cometh unto my people; for, notwithstanding the pains of my soul, I have seen it; wherefore, I know that it shall come to pass; and they sell themselves for naught; for, for the reward of their pride and their foolishness they shall reap destruction; for because they yield unto the devil and choose works of darkness rather than light, therefore they must go down to hell.
>
> 11 For the Spirit of the Lord will not always strive with man. And when the Spirit ceaseth to strive with man then cometh speedy destruction, and this grieveth my soul. (2 Nephi 26:10–11)

As we might expect if the setting were correct, all the various geographic descriptions noted in the Book of Mormon can be laid out in the western New York setting perfectly—a region not more than eighty miles from the Hill Cumorah itself where Nephi's prophecy proved to be true, when the Nephites and the Lamanites fought a final battle nine hundred years later around the Hill Cumorah. The Lamanites were the victors because the Nephites had become so steeped in sin that they were ripe for destruction.

Celtic Immigrants

Some of the blame for the destruction of the Nephites can also be laid at the feet of foreign immigrants from the north Atlantic Isles who brought the magic arts with them to the promised land. This should not be surprising since Satan could not sit idly by and watch the Lord's work continue unopposed. Ancient scripts found along the New England coast point to the arrival of Celtic tribes from Ireland and Iberia in the early centuries before Christ. Unfortunately, the Celts were pagans, while their Nephite neighbors were Christians. Once settled, the Celts built villages and temples and raised sacred circles, with monuments to both an older Mother Goddess and the pagan god—Bel or Baal. Their Druid priests instructed the locals in the area (many of which were Nephites) in the worship of the sun, the moon, and the stars and their influence on their lives, their agricultural pursuits, and their prospects for their futures.

A Celtic presence was found in Pennsylvania, just to the south of the Nephites and the Lamanites who were living in northern Pennsylvania and neighboring southern New York. This presence no doubt led to many of the false forms of worship and the anti-Christs that the scriptures said arrived among them from time to time, such as Nehor and Korihor (see Alma 1 and 30).

False Worship

False worship ultimately penetrated Nephite territory, which led to a list of sins. This caused pride, greed, and every other abomination to follow. These sins became all too easy to indulge in once they forgot the Lord and began to follow the dictates of Satan instead, just as Cain, the wicked antediluvian world, and the apostate Jaredites had done. Satan had a heyday with the Nephites, enticing them to indulge in every wicked thing he could conjure up to destroy the people of God. He used witchcraft and magic, and with all too much success. In time, their wickedness brought them to the brink of destruction, and the Lord had withdrawn His Spirit from them. Their cries for deliverance did not work this time, however, for their half-hearted attempts to repent were not sincere. Thus, the Lord permitted their enemies to destroy them.

> 10 And it came to pass that the Nephites began to repent of their
> iniquity, and began to cry even as had been prophesied by Samuel the

prophet; for behold no man could keep that which was his own, for the thieves, and the robbers, and the murderers, and the magic art, and the witchcraft which was in the land.

13 But behold this my joy was vain, for their sorrowing was not unto repentance, because of the goodness of God; but it was rather the sorrowing of the damned, because the Lord would not always suffer them to take happiness in sin. (Mormon 2:10, 13)

The Epilogue of a Nation

In the sad hours and years that followed the horrific battle at Cumorah, Moroni recorded not only the epilogue to his own people's destruction, but the fate that befell the Jaredites as well. In so doing, he was quick to remind us that their destruction came about because they had forsaken the Lord and had all turned to sin. The Nephites had also been duly warned by Nephi of the terrible consequences that would befall them if they turned from God after being led to the promised land: "Wherefore, this land is consecrated unto him whom he shall bring. And if it so be that they shall serve him according to the commandments which he hath given, it shall be a land of liberty unto them; wherefore, they shall never be brought down into captivity; if so, it shall be because of iniquity; for if iniquity shall abound cursed shall be the land for their sakes, but unto the righteous it shall be blessed forever" (2 Nephi 1:7).

A year before the Book of Mormon came off the press, the *Wayne Sentinel* published a few lines about the ancient race that mysteriously disappeared from New York's Finger Lakes region near Cumorah:

> There appears to be a gap in the history of the world, so far as relates to them [the ancient race], which can never be filled up. . . . We may picture them in our minds as a flourishing and mighty nation, possessing all the advantages and blessings of civil and religious liberty; powerful in wealth and natural resources; combining moral and political excellence; and seated upon the pinnacle of national prosperity and glory—and we may suppose that some dreadful plague, some natural calamity swept them from the face of the earth; or perhaps like Sodom and Gomorrah of old, their natural sins became so heinous, that the Almighty in his wrath utterly annihilated them; but after all our own conjectures. . . .
>
> Who they were and from whence they sprung . . . remains locked up in the womb of the past.[4]

How many missionaries would love to stand today and shout from the rooftops that their identity is not lost, nor is their history! It is a history preserved by holy prophets for the knowledge and benefit of our day; preserved so that we might know of the visit of Jesus Christ to this part of the world after His death and Resurrection, and that we learn from the lessons of the past and don't make the same mistakes that would unavoidably lead to our destruction as well. All the prophesied signs that herald the Second Coming of Christ speak of the destruction of the wicked prior to His glorious return.

The Statue Moroni

Only a quiet monument of the ancient prophet Moroni stands over the battlefields of Cumorah today—a tombstone of sorts, overlooking a land once covered with the dead and dying of two entire civilizations, having witnessed destruction in its most terrible form. Only the dry and rotting bones of the Nephites and the few relics found in their grave sites remain to tell the tale of their lives and times. Oh, if that statue could speak. After a fashion it does, for his story and that of his countrymen is found in The Book of Mormon, Another Testament of Jesus Christ.

Evidence of Warfare

During the early days of European colonization, before the encroachments of civilization obliterated all evidence of the destruction of the Nephites in western New York, O. Turner said,

> We are surrounded by evidence that a race preceded the present Indians, farther advanced in civilization and the arts, and far more numerous. Here and there upon the brow of hills, at the head of ravines, are their fortifications, their location selected with skill and adapted to refuge, subsistence and defense. Uprooted trees of the forest that are the growth of many centuries, expose their moulding remains, the uncovered mounds with masses of their skeletons promiscuously heaped one on top of the other, as if they were the gathered and hurriedly entombed dead of well contested battlefields. . . .
>
> Although not confined to this region, there is perhaps no portion of the United States where ancient relics are more numerous. Commencing near Oswego River, they extend westwardly over all the western counties of the state. . . . Then as now the western portion of New York state had attractions and inducements to make it a favorite

> residence, or this ancient people, . . . made this their refuge in a war of extermination. . . . That here was war of extermination, we may well conclude, from masses of human skeletons we find indiscriminately thrown together, indicating a common and simultaneous sepulchre from which age, infancy, sex and no condition, was exempt.[5]

The regions around the Hill Cumorah are filled with ten thousand small drumlin hills—small cigar-shaped hills of glacial till that were created when the great glaciers of the last Ice Age pressed over the region. The Hill Cumorah is one of many such hills in western and central New York that were fortified against the enemy during the Nephites' final days. In his research of the region for the Smithsonian Institution, E. G. Squier found numerous of these fortified sites extending from the counties of St. Lawrence in the north, to Chautauqua in the south, and embracing the counties of Jefferson, Oswego, Onondaga, Oneida, Cayuga, Seneca, Ontario, Wayne, Monroe, Livingston, Orleans, Niagara, Erie, Genesee, Cattaraugus, and Allegany. Squier noted more than one thousand sites in the Ontario, Livingston, Genesee, and Monroe counties alone, with nearly five hundred sites in Monroe County, and over one hundred fortified hilltops and strongholds in Genesee County.[6]

From *The Life of Heber C. Kimball, An Apostle*, by Orson F. Whitney, we read of Elder Kimball's exploration of the Cumorah lands in New York, where the bones of the ancient Nephites were whispering from the dust. He said,

> In the towns of Bloomfield, Victor, Manchester, and in the regions round about, there were hills upon the tops of which were entrenchments and fortifications, and in them were human bones, axes, tomahawks, points of arrows, beads and pipes, which were frequently found; and it was a common occurrence in the country to plow up axes, which I have done many times myself.
>
> I have visited the fortifications on the tops of those hills frequently, and the one near Bloomfield I have crossed hundreds of times, which is on the bluff of Honeyoye River, at the outlet of Honeyoye Lake. . . .
>
> The Hill Cumorah is a high hill for that country, and had the appearance of a fortification or entrenchment around it. In the State of New York, probably there are hundreds of these fortifications which are now visible. . . .
>
> Readers of the Book of Mormon will remember that in this very region, according to that sacred record, the final battles were

> fought between the Nephites and Lamanites. At the hill Cumorah, the Nephites made their last stand prior to their utter destruction, A.D. 385.[7]

No other region in the Americas provides more evidence of ancient warfare than western New York—an area that the Lamanites held in their control until the times of the Gentiles.

Joseph Smith Identifies the Promised Land and Its Inhabitants

In the Wentworth Letter, Joseph Smith attempted to explain his mission of bringing about the ancient record of the inhabitants of this country. In referring to the angel Moroni's recital about the aborigines of this country (meaning the Native Americans), he said the following:

> I was also informed concerning the aboriginal inhabitants of this country and shown who they were, and from whence they came; a brief sketch of their origin, progress, civilization, laws, governments, of their righteousness and iniquity, and the blessings of God being finally withdrawn from them as a people, was made known unto me; I was also told where were deposited some plates on which were engraven an abridgment of the records of the ancient Prophets that had existed on this continent. . . .
>
> In this important and interesting book the history of ancient America is unfolded, from its first settlement by a colony that came from the Tower of Babel, at the confusion of languages to the beginning of the fifth century of the Christian Era. We are informed by these records that America in ancient times has been inhabited by two distinct races of people. The first were called Jaredites, and came directly from the Tower of Babel. The second race came directly from the city of Jerusalem about six hundred years before Christ. They were principally Israelites, of the descendants of Joseph.[8]

Conclusion

It can hardly be doubted that our own blessed America is the land spoken of by the ancient prophets because the *stick of Joseph* deals exclusively with the events that transpired in America—more specifically amid the hills and valleys of western New York. While the Nephites spread out into a number of other regions, the story of the

Nephites' long sojourn in the promised and began in this region, and after nine centuries of intrigue and warfare, ended there as well.

During that long span of time, righteous men were raised up to record the history of their day, to preserve for us a legacy of prophecy and religious insights worthy of our attention and instruction, and to impress upon our minds that only those who worship God will prosper in the promised land.

The Nephite saga is of paramount importance in the overall picture of the coming of Christ. It was Moroni himself, the last Nephite prophet, who gave the golden record of his people over to Joseph Smith for translation. This thereby restored the Lord's gospel in its fulness, as is mentioned in Revelation's end times prophecy:

> 6 And I saw another angel fly in the midst of heaven, having the everlasting gospel to preach unto them that dwell on the earth, and to every nation, and kindred, and tongue, and people,
>
> 7 Saying with a loud voice, Fear God, and give glory to him; for the hour of his judgment is come: and worship him that made heaven, and earth, and the sea, and the fountains of waters. (Revelation 14:6–7)

Notes

1. *Wikipedia*, s.v. "Proto-Algonquian language," last modified January 8, 2017, en.wikipedia.org/wiki/Proto-Algonquian_language.
2. William A. Ritchie, *The Archaeology of New York State*, rev. ed. (New York: Natural History Press, 1997), 208.
3. Ibid.
4. E. Cecil McGavin and Willard Bean, *The Geography of the Book of Mormon*, 2nd ed. (Salt Lake City: Bookcraft, 1949), 61.
5. Ibid., 63.
6. Ibid., 65.
7. Orson F. Whitney, *The Life of Heber C. Kimball* (Salt Lake City: Bookcraft, 1973), 25.
8. Joseph Smith, in *History of the Church*, 4:537.

4

The Wide Distribution of the Lamanites

The Lamanites will be among those who will also hear and embrace the gospel once the plan of salvation is reintroduced to them in the latter days. With the scriptures making it clear that Lehi's seed was given the land of promise as an eternal inheritance, we would do well to identify the survivors of the terrible battle at Cumorah—namely, the Lamanites. The Lamanites took full control of the land once they destroyed their Nephite brothers in 385 BC. While the Lamanites also paid a dear price in the loss of lives and property, their seed was preserved by the Lord from total destruction in deference to various Nephite prophets who pled with the Lord on their behalf. The prophet Enos was one of those Nephite prophets who, in recording his commune with God (where he received a remission of his own sins), said,

> 9 Now, it came to pass that when I had heard these words I began to feel a desire for the welfare of my brethren, the Nephites; wherefore, I did pour out my whole soul unto God for them.
>
> 10 And while I was thus struggling in the spirit, behold, the voice of the Lord came into my mind again, saying: I will visit thy brethren according to their diligence in keeping my commandments. I have given unto them this land, and it is a holy land; and I curse it not save it be for the cause of iniquity; wherefore, I will visit thy brethren according as I have said; and their transgressions will I bring down with sorrow upon their own heads.

11 And after I, Enos, had heard these words, my faith began to be unshaken in the Lord; and I prayed unto him with many long strugglings for my brethren, the Lamanites.

12 And it came to pass that after I had prayed and labored with all diligence, the Lord said unto me: I will grant unto thee according to thy desires, because of thy faith.

13 And now behold, this was the desire which I desired of him—that if it should so be, that my people, the Nephites, should fall into transgression, and by any means be destroyed, and the Lamanites should not be destroyed, that the Lord God would preserve a record of my people, the Nephites; even if it so be by the power of his holy arm, that it might be brought forth at some future day unto the Lamanites, that, perhaps, they might be brought unto salvation. (Enos 1:9–13)

Identifying the Lamanites of the Book of Mormon

Depending solely on what little DNA evidence could be gleaned from the remains of America's ancient residents, early theories over the past century had all Native American DNA falling within four haplogroups: A, B, C, and D. Three of the four haplogroups are found primarily in Asia. Thus, with no new evidence to suggest otherwise, the theory that America was peopled primarily by tribes migrating from Asia was perpetuated throughout the generations. However, when a rare genetic DNA link called haplogroup X was discovered among the North American tribes, scholars suggested the possibility that some of the Native American founders were of Caucasian origins and arrived via an Atlantic crossing rather than a Pacific one. It has been firmly established that the haplogroup X2 originated in the Palestinian territories—in Mesopotamia, the Caucasus, Syria, Lebanon, Jordan, Cyprus, and Israel. The Algonquian of the American northeast carry the X haplogroup at frequencies as high as 10–40 percent, particularly the Ojibway, who carry it at 25 percent, as do the Iroquois. It is as high as 15 percent among the Sioux brothers of the Iroquois, with the Nuu-chah-nulth in the American northwest carrying it at a frequency of 11–13 percent. The Navajo in Arizona, Utah, and New Mexico carry it at 7 percent, while the Yakima of Washington carry it at frequencies of 5 percent.[1] Thus, it is obvious that the X haplogroup, found in

North America, diminished in frequencies the farther west it travels, which strengthens the hypothesis of an Atlantic crossing.

THE IROQUOIS

Although several related tribes across the country carry the X haplogroup, it is found more frequently in the regions around the Great Lakes than elsewhere in North America. The Great Lakes area is dominated by the Algonquian-speaking people, and also the Iroquois who provide the clearest link to the Lamanites carrying the seed of Lehi. It is now the common consensus that the Iroquois developed right there in New York from the ancestral Point Peninsula populations of 600 BC into the later Owasco culture, and ultimately into the Iroquois.[2] The Proto-Iroquois language is linked to the Allegheny Range, which includes the southern tier of New York State in Chautauqua and Cattaraugus counties—the proposed land of Nephi. During more recent historic times, Iroquois war parties reportedly roamed over half of America and their name instilled terror from the Atlantic to the Mississippi. Thus, it appears that this people retained the same dispositions as their Lamanite forefathers who wiped out the entire Nephite population around the Hill Cumorah centuries earlier, leaving the Lamanites in sole possession of New York.

By the time of European colonization, the Iroquois occupied territory covering a vast area. Toward the south, they occupied territory along the north shores of Chesapeake Bay, where their fathers first landed after their long ocean voyage. Traveling west, they could be found in Kentucky and onward to the confluence of the Ohio and Mississippi River; northward, up the Illinois River and into Michigan; east, across lower Michigan and southern Ontario and parts of Quebec; south, into northern New England; westward, to the Connecticut River and the Hudson and upper Delaware Valleys; and across Pennsylvania and back again to Chesapeake Bay—right where their forefathers first made landfall.

THE CHEROKEE

The Cherokee are the southernmost branch of the Iroquois nation and are considered to be the largest and most important tribe in the southeast (although their beginnings were farther north). From their initial strongholds in northern Pennsylvania and southwestern New York, some of the Lamanite descendants came to settle the Allegheny

River, a major tributary of the Ohio River. They were originally known as the Allegewi—named after the river. It would be many centuries later that they became known as the Cherokee. Formerly, they had the whole mountain region of the southern Alleghenies in their control in southwest Virginia, western North Carolina, South Carolina, northern Georgia, eastern Tennessee, northeastern Alabama, and Ohio. While the Cherokee exhibit similar haplogroup frequencies with both the northern Iroquois and the southeastern Muskogean groups with which they intermarried, they are considered by all to be the southernmost branch of the Iroquois. Recent research revealed the X haplogroup in several modern Cherokee. Genetic testing done among those who proved to have a high degree of interrelatedness and common ancestral lines showed the T haplogroup to be the largest, followed by U, X, J, and H, all of which are noted in populations of Egypt, Israel, and the Near East.

THE SIOUX

According to the *Glossary of Indian Nations*, Siouan is a language group that is also believed to be related to the Iroquoian language.[3] The Sioux are the largest and most important Indian tribe north of Mexico, with the single exception of the Ojibway. While the Sioux were more numerous in the West, linguistic and other evidence has led to the common belief that they originated in the East. An aged chief of the Osage branch of the Sioux revealed to a Mr. Gravier in 1701,

> That the tradition had been steadily handed down by their ancestors that [they] had originally emigrated from the east, because the population had become too numerous for their hunting grounds. He described the forks of the Alleghany and Monongahela rivers and the falls of the Ohio at Louisville, where he said they had dwelt some time, and where large bands had separated from them and distributed themselves throughout the surrounding country. Those who did not remain in the region of the Ohio followed its waters until they reached the mouth, and then ascended to the mouth of the Missouri, where other separations took place, some going northward up the Mississippi, others advancing up the waters of the Missouri.[4]

Sioux traditions also have some of their people moving south and east into the Appalachia regions of Virginia, West Virginia, Kentucky, North and South Carolina, Georgia, Florida, and Louisiana. Still others moved west across the Mississippi to the Great Plains; others moved south through Texas and north to the Canadian border where they are known respectively as the Lakota and Dakota. In total, the Siouan language family encompassed over two million square miles, covering regions in Missouri, Arkansas, Iowa, Illinois, Minnesota, Wisconsin, Nebraska, Kansas, North Dakota, South Dakota, Wyoming, Montana, Idaho, and Colorado. From this mother tongue, their language evolved into over 104 different languages, with the Sioux still speaking of themselves as the "people of the parent speech." Thus, while the heartland of the saga of the Book of Mormon took place in only the limited region of New York, the descendants of Lehi ultimately filled up half of America, where they remain to this day.

The Algonquian Connection

The Algonquian have a physiological characteristic: a round- or brachycephalic-skull type typical of the tribe of Judah. This skull type can be tied to the Mulekites, who occupied lower Ontario where the Algonquian language originated long before the Nephites joined them in Zarahemla. The Nephites, on the other hand, had a dolichocephalic- or long-skull type typical of the other tribes of Israel. Once the two people merged, a new skull type evolved called mesocephalic. The Algonquians (living westward across the Upper Great Lakes and north into Canada) are shown to have both a round- or mesocephalic-skull type and thus are tied more to Mulek's line.

The Point Peninsula culture of western New York in 600 BC (the Nephites and the Mulekites) took in a wide range, with the Mulekites living in northwestern New York and lower Ontario for several centuries before the Nephites joined them. The Mulekites moved primarily from western New York into Lower Ontario and all through the upper Great Lakes because they were a trading people and used the lakes as highways. The Algonquian language family is believed to have originated in lower Ontario between 2,500 and 3,000 years ago, which was precisely when the Mulekites would have arrived. The Nephites, on the other hand, show evidence of living to the south of Mulekites in southwestern New York before merging with them in Zarahemla (located in western New York in an area now occupied by the modern city of Buffalo—the second largest city in New York, second only to New York City).

Around 46 BC, the Book of Mormon has a large number of Nephites moving from Zarahemla along the north shores of Lake Erie into the land northward (the fertile plains along the southern shores of Lake Ontario around the lands of Cumorah—home of the earlier Jaredites whose large population formerly stripped the land of its timber). A journey of 125 miles (an exceedingly long distance) would have taken the Nephites from Zarahemla at the north end of Lake Erie—north and east to central New York's "land of many waters." This land is where we find the Finger Lakes today (eleven long fingers of water), with the northern ends of the lakes being the most heavily occupied anciently. Helaman describes that migration for us. We read:

> 3 And it came to pass in the forty and sixth, yea, there was much contention and many dissensions; in the which there were an exceedingly great many who departed out of the land of Zarahemla, and went forth unto the land northward to inherit the land.
>
> 4 And they did travel to an exceedingly great distance, insomuch that they came to large bodies of water and many rivers.
>
> 5 Yea, and even they did spread forth into all parts of the land, into whatever parts it had not been rendered desolate and without timber, because of the many inhabitants who had before inherited the land. . . .
>
> 12 And it came to pass that there were many of the people of Ammon, who were Lamanites by birth, did also go forth into this land.
>
> 13 And now there are many records kept of the proceedings of this people, by many of this people, which are particular and very large, concerning them.
>
> 14 But behold, a hundredth part of the proceedings of this people, yea, the account of the Lamanites and of the Nephites, and their wars, and contentions, and dissensions, and their preaching, and their prophecies, and their shipping and their building of ships, and their building of temples, and of synagogues and their sanctuaries, and their righteousness, and their wickedness, and their murders, and their robbings, and their plundering, and all manner of abominations and whoredoms, cannot be contained in this work.
>
> 15 But behold, there are many books and many records of every kind, and they have been kept chiefly by the Nephites.
>
> 16 And they have been handed down from one generation to another by the Nephites, even until they have fallen into transgression and have been murdered, plundered, and hunted, and driven forth, and slain, and scattered upon the face of the earth, and mixed with the Lamanites until they are no more called the Nephites, becoming wicked, and

> wild, and ferocious, yea, even becoming Lamanites. (Helaman 3:3–5, 12–16)

It is commonly believed that the Iroquois evolved right there in New York from the earlier Point Peninsula populations. Their influence was felt among all the tribes from Lake Erie eastward to Lake Onondaga at the east end of the Finger Lakes. It would be here that they would form their now famous Iroquois League (also known as the "Five Nations" and the later as the "Six Nations"). These were a people who had prophets among them just like the Nephites did, perhaps those with ties to the children of Ammon (those Lamanites converted by Ammon).

Continued Migration

Although the heaviest populations of the Nephites and Lamanites who moved north remained in New York, the archaeological record shows that the Point Peninsula people carried their culture farther north up the St. Lawrence River shortly before the time of Christ. This movement allowed them to settle around Lake Champlain and across Maine, New Hampshire, and New Brunswick—all part of their promised land of inheritance. The southern range of the Point Peninsula populations, which, by now, consisted chiefly of Lamanites (Iroquois), spread eastward across the entire southern tier of New York State to New England.[5] The Lamanites did not merge as a body with the Mulekites like the Nephites did, having remained chiefly in southwestern New York and Pennsylvania. Thus, their language was different than the northern Algonquians (which were of chiefly Mulekite origins)—a language the Nephites could not even understand when they first joined them, for their language had become corrupted (see Omni 1:17). As the merger of the two people took place, the Nephites taught the Mulekites their language. Various dialects emerged because it had been three or four hundred years since their arrival in the land, and the Mulekites were now scattered all across the upper Great Lakes and into Canada. Another hundred years would find the Nephites migrating east to the Atlantic—both the Nephites and the Mulekites were part of the same ancestral family of Jacob (the great patriarch of Israel). Early explorers would come to call them Algic: a generic term for those of the Algonquian language family. Today the Algonquian language is divided into three subgroups: the Central Algonquian language family, the Plains Algonquians (for those who settled farther west), and the Eastern Algonquians along the Atlantic coast. Thus, many of our Algonquian tribes today carry both Mulekite and Nephite blood. The blood of Judah through Mulek predominates among those around the Great Lakes, while Nephite blood predominates in the east.

Skull Types

While the website *Access Genealogy* describes the Algonquians living around the Great Lakes as having an almost brachycephalic- or round-skull type, they speak of those along the Atlantic coast as being tall with heads that were much more elongated—the same skull type found among the Iroquois (the true remnants of the Lamanites), who carried the skull type of Joseph's line through Lehi. Moreover, they carry the X haplogroup with ties to Israel, and are prone to the long- or dolichocephalic-skull type typical of the Nephites. The Delaware branch of the Algonquians is the most dolichocephalic of them all. The scriptures clearly state that of those who moved north it was chiefly the Nephites that kept their records. We can now equate those with the Ojibway and Micmac living along the Atlantic coast whose writing style is very much like the hieroglyphic writing found on the characters transcript from which the Book of Mormon was translated.

The Ojibway

The Ojibway are one of most prominent members of Algic stock and are the most numerous of all the divisions of aboriginal tribes of North America. William Warren, who spent many years among the Ojibway, wrote:

> The more I have become acquainted with their anomalous and difficult to be understand characters—the more insight I have gained into their religious and secret rites and faith, the more strongly has it been impressed on my mind that they bear a close affinity or analogy to the chosen people of God, and they are either descendants of the lost tribes of Israel, or they have had, in some former era, a close contact and intercourse with Hebrews, imbibing from them their beliefs and customs and the traditions of their patriarchs.[6]

Pocahontas Was an Eastern Algonquian (Nephite)

When European explorers first arrived in New England, the paramount chief of the Algonquians living in Virginia—Powhatan—held dominion over an area that covered six thousand square miles and included thirty Algonquian nations. This made his domain the largest of all the Algonquian confederacies. Thus the Indians who first greeted our pilgrim fathers on the rocky coast of Massachusetts carried Nephite blood, as were those who met William Penn. Even the Indian princess, Pocahontas, was of Eastern Algonquian stock. We know they were of Nephite descent because it was the Nephites that kept the records of those who moved north (such as the Ojibway and Micmac), and the Eastern Algonquian DNA includes the X haplogroup.

The Seed of Lehi among the Gentiles of Early Colonial America

We often consider Columbus to be the Gentile noted in the scriptures who is said to have come upon the seed of Lehi when Europeans first arrived in the New World. Yet, while Columbus opened the way for ongoing exploration, he never made it to North America. It was John Cabot who first landed along the east coast of America and found Nephi's descendants living along the Atlantic coast of New England, "And I looked and beheld a man among the Gentiles, who was separated from the seed of my brethren by the many waters; and I beheld the Spirit of God, that it came down and wrought upon the man; and he went forth upon the many waters, even unto the seed of my brethren, who were in the promised land" (1 Nephi 13:12).

The descendants of Lehi (through both the Eastern Algonquian and southern Iroquois tribes) occupied all of the original thirteen United States colonies.

US State	Native American Tribes
Connecticut	Mochican
Delaware	Lenni Lenape
Georgia	Cherokee
Maine	Wampanoag, Micmac, Abenaki
Maryland	Susquehannock
Massachusetts	Wampanoag, Micmac, Abenaki
New Hampshire	Abenaki
New Jersey	Lenni Lenape
New York	Iroquois, Algonquian
North Carolina	Cherokee, Catawba branch of the Sioux
Pennsylvania	Shawnee, Seneca
Rhode Island	Narragansett, Nipmuc
South Carolina	Cherokee
Virginia	Powhatan[7]

Micmac Hieroglyphic Writing

Both the Ojibway and Micmac kept written records of their people on birch bark scrolls. The Nephites' ancient hieroglyphic style of writing perpetuated by those in the north was first recognized in 1610 when Catholic monks began to teach the aboriginal tribes of the region about Christianity. But, while teaching them, they became aware that the Micmac wrote in a form of Egyptian hieroglyphics, which has led to a considerable amount of controversy over the years. However, after extensive study of the Micmac hieroglyphics, the epigrapher Barry Fell could see a definite connection between the Algonquians and the Egyptians, and firmly believed that someone familiar with the Egyptian hieroglyphic system had to have contrived the Micmac writing.[8]

The Book of Mormon addresses that subject as well. Moroni writes, "And now, behold, we have written this record according to our knowledge, in the characters which are called among us the reformed Egyptian, being handed down and altered by us, according to our manner of speech" (Mormon 9:32).

Prophetic Warnings Given to the Descendants of Nephi

In Jacob 3:1–4, we learn that the Lord fully intended to lead the righteous out from among the wicked Nephites before their final days of reckoning (with the righteous Lamanites no doubt included in that promise). The people of Ammon (meaning those of the Lamanites who were converted to the gospel of Christ) were among those who left Zarahemla between 49 BC and 39 BC and headed north. Thus the Lord appears to have preserved the more righteous branches of Lehi's family for His own wise purposes. He preserved both the Nephites and the Lamanites, with those thus preserved destined to carry further warnings to those of our day who may be falling into wicked ways. The Book of Mormon details prophecies of men of God who were guided by the Spirit to warn and forewarn the seed of Lehi of impeding struggles based on their behavior. These prophecies were destined to impact not only their own lives, but the lives of their Lamanite descendants living far in the future as well. Mormon said, "I also know that as many things as have been prophesied concerning us down to this day have been fulfilled, and as many as go beyond this day must surely come to pass" (Words of Mormon 1:4). Thus, the prophecies of the Lamanite descendants will be included in this work, along with those of our Latter-day prophets. The two will blend together to provide an even clearer picture of the events yet to come.

Notes

1. Maere Reidla et. al., "Origin and Diffusion of mtDNA haplogroup X," *The American Journal of Human Genetics* 73, (2003), 1178–90. doi:10.1086/379380. See also Ripan S. Malhi, Beth A. Schultx, David Glenn Smith, "Distribution of Mitochondrial DNA Lineages among Native American Tribes of Northeastern North America," *Human Biology* 73, no. 1, (February 2001), 17–55. doi:10.1353/hub.2001.0008.
2. William A. Ritchie, *The Archaeology of New York State* (Garden City, NY: The Natural History Press, 1965).
3. *Glossary of Indian Nations*, s.v. "Siouan," accessed March 23, 2017, www.hotcakencyclopedia.com/ho.GlossaryIndianNations .html. See also Carl Waldman, *Encyclopedia of Native American Tribes*, rev. ed. (New York: Checkmark Books, 1999).
4. "Siouan Migrations and Iroquois Conquests," *Access Genealogy*, accessed March 15, 2017, www.accessgenealogy.com/native /siouan-migrations-and-iroquois-conquests.htm.
5. William A. Ritchie, *The Archaeology of New York State*, rev. ed. (New York: Natural History Press, 1997), 208.
6. William Warren, *History of the Ojibway People* (Minnesota Historical Society Press, 1984), 63.
7. "Original Inhabitants of the 13 Colonies," *United States History*, accessed March 23, 2017, www.u-s-history.com/pages/h936 .html.
8. Barry Fell, *America B. C.: Ancient Settlers in the New World* (Muskogee, OK: Artisan Publishers, 1989), 256–57.

5

The Southern Tribes of Ancient America

The Nahuatl tribes lived farther south, bordering the Gulf of Mexico. Yet they too appear to have ties to Israel. We might remember that Judah had two sons, one called Perez and the other Zarah, or Zerah. These ties to Israel come through Zarah, the twin brother of Perez, who fathered the ancestors of the Mulekites. The story of the birth of Judah's twin boys is well known, with Zarah being known as the *son of the scarlet thread*, for it was his little hand that emerged from the womb first. A scarlet thread was attached to his wrist to show his birthright as the first born of Judah. However, in the process of birth, Zarah pulled his hand back in and Perez emerged first, not Zarah. Thus, a breach had taken place in the royal line, and Perez was declared the rightful heir of the royal house of David (see Genesis 38:27–30).

Because both boys were princes of the royal house of Judah, some have suggested that while the line of Perez was destined to provide the royal kings for the house of David through which the Savior would come, perhaps the twins were to rule jointly, with Zarah's line providing a line of kings for various other regions Israel was destined to settle. Scriptural evidence indicates that some of the Zarahites remained with Israel, yet other descendants appear to have left the main congregation and founded and ruled the cities of Athens, Troy, and Miletus—cities filled with two prominent lines of Israel, one from Zarah and the other from the tribe of Dan. Various ancient historians have placed Danite sea-merchants all along the Mediterranean Sea. Large numbers of these sea-merchants settled ancient Greece, and they came to be known as Spartans. Just to the east of the Mediterranean in western Turkey (or Anatolia), lay the ancient city of Troy, where many also settled among the royal line of their Hebrew cousin Zarah. After the fall of Troy in 1200 BC, the house of Zarah-Judah went on to father various lines of kings throughout Western Europe, including England, Scandinavia, the Isles of the Atlantic, and apparently southeastern America and Mexico as well.[1]

Their identities can be traced back to the Old World via DNA with a fair amount of accuracy. It seems that the native races of the American southeast carry a predominance of the Q haplogroup normally found among the people of Anatolia in western Turkey. Anatolia is the place of the ancient city of Troy where the locals (who the Trojans married) were fathered by Togarmah, the only grandson of Japheth to carry the Q haplogroup. By examining the language, culture, and architecture of those in Greece, and of those in neighboring Illyria and Bosnia (where the Bosnian temples of the sun and moon match those in Mexico much better than the ones in Egypt), it has become more and more evident that the Nahuatl races who first settled in southeastern America were part of fleeing Zarah and Danite fleets. One fleet arrived off the coast of America (probably in Florida) around 279 BC—the very date given for the Celtic invasion of Greece, which sent so many Danites and Zarahites (who were living in Macedonia) fleeing for their lives. Many sailed off in Danite ships for parts unknown.[2] Mesoamerican traditions all point to white people with beards "who crossed the Atlantic and made fundament[al] contributions to the diffusion of culture . . . to Mesoamerica and . . . parts of the southern half of North America."[3] Both Mayan and Aztec tradition tell of these "white gods" arriving with predictions from astronomers, architects, and priests.

The Southwestern Hopi Connection

No origins have yet been given for the Hopi other than to suggest that they descended from the ancestral Puebloan enemies of the Navaho. Various theories about their origins have surfaced over the years. Gene Matlock ties them to the subcontinent of India where traditions have their people visiting and colonizing America right up until colonial times. Certain legends among the Anasazi and Hopi appear to substantiate that theory. A few Hindu scholars have even tied Hopi religious traditions to India, suggesting that they were likely transmitted across the sea by Danite seamen, also called Naga, which means serpent (the tribal symbol of Dan is the serpent and *naga* means snake or serpent).[4]

Danite Seamen

Various historians follow the seafaring Danites to Carthage in North Africa and from there across the Mediterranean Sea to Greece. Yet others note that they merged with Scythian sea-merchants who traversed even greater distances. For instance, Matlock tells us that the Naga maritime people also once inhabited the areas of what are now Afghanistan, Tibet, Pakistan, and northwestern India.[5] Thus, these Naga Danites carried the blood of Israel far and wide, and not surprisingly, for they were destined to do so. When Moses gave his final blessing to the children of Israel, he prophesied that Dan would be as a lion's whelp who would leap from Bashan (see Deuteronomy 33:22). This suggests that his tribe would journey forth by *leaps*. One great leap took place when the Danites merged with the Scythians (moving southward into Afghanistan, Pakistan, Tibet, and northwestern India) where they became a rich, maritime people who are often referred to as white Hindus. These Hindu-Danites were the children of the *Mother Goddess Danu* whose serpent children ruled the waters and settled many lands carrying the Hindu religion with them. Matlock claims that these Naga serpents were a highly civilized ruling maritime and mercantile class who founded colonies scattered all over southeast Asia, the South Pacific, Mexico, and Central and South America. They carried the Hindu religion with them, much of which revolves around serpent worship.[6] Thus, it is no surprise to note a connection between the Hopi, Maya, and the Hindu Buddhist. Nor should it be a surprise that the Hopi and Maya calendar and many of their prophecies are the same as that of the Hindus.

DNA

While the origins of the Hopi have not yet been reconciled, haplogroup frequencies in the ancient remains of American southwestern Anasazi and their descending Hopi is typified by high levels of the B haplogroup, moderate frequencies of the C haplogroup, and low frequencies of the X haplogroup. However, while both haplogroup B and C attain their highest frequencies among the indigenous populations of Mongolia and the Russian Far East, it displays its highest diversity among modern populations of India. The X haplogroup is found in ancient Israel, which in this case was likely an admixture from Dan.

Ancestral and Cultural Ties

The tribe of Dan has always been associated with the serpent, for the serpent was the symbol given to Dan while he was still living among the other twelve tribes of Israel (each of which was given a symbol of their own). As mentioned before, the term *naga* means serpent in India.[7] Gene D. Matlock, in his book *India Once Ruled the Americas*, maintains that a man named Kuvera, a brilliant deified Phoenician sea king, or Naga King, learned how to smelt copper, gold, and other metals in a mountainous region of southwestern Afghanistan and northeastern Pakistan. His own kingdom, according to Hindu mythology, was located on a barren peak in Western Tibet.[8] Originally, these Phoenician Nagas were not a land-based people, but rather a maritime power with the ocean said to be their habitat. We find the same description in numerous references to the seafaring exploits of the Danites, who, together with the Phoenicians, sailed many seas. An ancient legend from India has it that Kadru, the mother of the serpents, compelled an eagle or hawk "to serve her sons by transporting them across the sea to a beautiful country in a distant land, which was inhabited by other Nagas," for the Nagas were expert navigators and had founded colonies upon a number of distant coasts.[9] It should no longer be doubted that many people arrived in America from both sides—from China and India on one side, and Europe and the north Atlantic on the other. The Nagas, or the serpent people of the Indus River Valley in India, were no doubt perfectly capable of making it to America.

The Gods of the Hopi

The creation myths of the Hopi center around Tawa, the sun spirit, or Great Spirit, who formed the earth out of endless space—something also noted in Hebrew mythology. But from there things change. The Hopi add a mother goddess to the pantheon, as well as a nephew called Sotuknang who is said to be the god who intercedes between humans and Tawa (not Jehovah, the son of God). They also believed in Masauwu, or Massau, the god of both the underworld and earth who is said to wear a hideous mask. Masauwu made it perfectly clear to the Hopi that he was the master of the upper world—the Earth God—and that all the land from north to south and east to west belonged to him. The Hopi say he was not permitted to walk the land in the daytime, but only at night guided by the light of the fire. He is the proclaimed door keeper of the world of the Hopi. While he is often described as being a bloody, fearsome creature, the Hopi say he is really a very handsome man—a giant with fine black hair who goes about in animal skins when moving about the upper world.[10]

From the *Book of the Hopi*, we learn that Masauwu appeared to the Hopi at the emergence of the Fourth World. The people recognized him; he had been appointed head caretaker of the Third World, but becoming a little self-important, had lost his humility before the Creator. Being a spirit, Masauwu could not die, so Tawa took his appointment away from him and made Masauwu the deity of death and the underworld. This job below was not as pleasant as the one above. Then, when the Third World was destroyed [during the Flood] Tawa decided to give Masauwu another chance, as he had given the people, and he appointed Masauwu to guard and protect this Fourth World as its caretaker.[11]

As caretaker of the earth, it was Masauwu who gave the Hopi permission to settle their lands in the Mesas, a vast desert region where they would have to depend upon him for the rainfall they needed to grow their crops. They would thus be required to invoke his assistance through constant petition, ceremony, and prayer. However, no one dared to watch those ceremonies that called upon Masauwu, especially if he appeared with the One Horned Priests who did his bidding in the underworld, and the spirits of the dead, for it is said that anyone who saw them would become so frozen with fear that they would appear to be dead.[12]

Hugh Nibley recorded a time when this evil man portrayed himself as the Messiah. Nibley referenced a time when a Hopi leader walked up a hill and saw Masauwu sitting there and asked who he was:

> He said, "I am Mashovi." The two names given are Mashow (Messiah) and Mashovi. He said "I am Mashovi, and I rule all this land that you can see. It all belongs to me as far as you can see. If you want to settle here, you must pay tithes to me." The leader put out his hand for the nakwatch; that's the sacred grip to identify himself. As the tall, handsome man put out his hand. The leader gave a strong jerk on it and pulled off his mask . . . , and it was a death head. It was Satan

> masquerading as the Messiah. Nevertheless, they still continue to pay their tithes to him, because after all he is the ruler of this world. He is the one who possesses the land. They will pay their tithes in the Church, but they will also pay their ten percent to Mashovi. The interesting thing is that the same story is told in Tha>lab *[sic]*, whom I failed to bring today, about when David went up to the mount of the temple in Jerusalem. He wanted to build a temple there. He was met by the tall, handsome stranger who was Satan and had to have a fight with him. It's a very interesting thing the way these tie up. This name Messiah is the name they would use for Christ.[13]

Some have suggested that a conspiracy existed between Satan and the tribe of Dan to steal the Messianic birthright from the tribe of Judah and establish a false Messiah—the anti-Christ of the latter days. The last mention of Dan in the Old Testament insinuates that he had a different god than the rest of Israel. It reads as follows:

> 11 Behold, the days come, saith the Lord God, that I will send a famine in the land, not a famine of bread, nor a thirst for water, but of hearing the words of the Lord:
>
> 12 And they shall wander from sea to sea, and from the north even to the east, they shall run to and fro to seek the word of the Lord, and shall not find it.
>
> 13 In that day shall the fair virgins and young men faint for thirst.
>
> 14 They that swear by the sin of Samaria, and say, Thy god, O Dan, liveth; and, The manner of Beer-sheba liveth; even they shall fall, and never rise up again. (Amos 8:11–14)

The Hopi are considered to be both ecologists and peacemakers. Their priesthood revolved around a form of nature worship, particularly the sun. All forms of nature were worshipped, including clouds, rain, springs, and streams. Their obvious reverence and worship of their dead also suggests that they indulged in ancestral worship. Their snake cult suggesting snake worship. The Hopi claim that it was their ancestors that built the serpent-shaped mounds found in eastern North America during their many years of wandering. Their capital city was ultimately centered at Chaco Canyon, New Mexico, which became the centralized political and religious center of the area. It had a complex network of roads linking hundreds of communities and population centers together. There have been roads noted among the outlying colonies of the Nahuatl races, particularly the Toltecs and the Aztecs living in southeastern America and northern Mexico.

> NOTE: As of 1982, only about 5 percent of all Hopi were Christians.[14] One report noted that only a dozen or so Hopi have been converted.[15]
>
> In 1847, the Mormons [The Church of Jesus Christ of Latter-day Saints] entered what is now Utah and began to proselytize the Utes, Paiutes, and Shoshones who traditionally lived in the area. Within a decade, the Mormon missionaries began to move south into present-day Arizona and to seek converts among the Hopi. Overall, the Mormon missionary work attracted only a few converts, but it was more successful than other Christian faiths.[16]

Language Ties to the Southeastern Tribes

The Hopi are descended from the ancestral Anasazi, but no one knows what language the Anasazi spoke. However, it is known that the Hopi spoke a language dialect tied to the Uto-Aztecan language group of the Nahuas, which may tie into their common ancestor. Mounting evidence suggests that the Four Corners region may even be the birthplace of the Aztec branch of the Nahuas, who ultimately made it southward into Mexico in the twelfth century. There they built up the famed Aztec Empire—one of the bloodiest and most corrupt empires ever to have existed. The Aztecs, Nahuas, and Toltecs are essentially all branches of the same family and all spoke dialects of the same language family, including the Hopi. Whether or not it was their mother tongue is not yet known, but trade routes back and forth between the Toltecs and Anasazi have been well documented. This suggests definite ties between the two people, and perhaps even genetic ties, for "It is reasonable to assume that where there is a linguistic relationship there is most likely also a genetic relationship."[17]

Prelude to Christ

With so many branches of Israel planted in America, and with the Savior's mortal ministry coming to an end, the stage was now set for the Lord's visit to His New World flock after His death and Resurrection. Yet only some of the Nephites, Lamanites, and Mulekites living in the northeast were living the doctrines of Christ and only they would be privileged to have such a visitation. All the others had carried pagan traditions with them into the land from the sun-worshiping cultures across the sea. Not even all the Nephites would be privileged to see and hear Him, only those who had been waiting for His prophesied appearance for years, not the more stiff-necked among them who refused to believe. Five years prior to the Lord's birth, the prophet Samuel said the following:

> 2 Behold, I give unto you a sign; for five years more cometh, and behold, then cometh the Son of God to redeem all those who shall believe on his name.
>
> 3 And behold, this will I give unto you for a sign at the time of his coming; for behold, there shall be great lights in heaven, insomuch that in the night before he cometh there shall be no darkness, insomuch that it shall appear unto man as if it was day.
>
> 4 Therefore, there shall be one day and a night and a day, as if it were one day and there were no night; and this shall be unto you for a sign; for ye shall know of the rising of the sun and also of its setting; therefore they shall know of a surety that there shall be two days and a night; nevertheless the night shall not be darkened; and it shall be the night before he is born.
>
> 5 And behold, there shall a new star arise, such an one as ye never have beheld; and this also shall be a sign unto you.
>
> 6 And behold this is not all, there shall be many signs and wonders in heaven.
>
> 7 And it shall come to pass that ye shall all be amazed, and wonder, insomuch that ye shall fall to the earth.
>
> 8 And it shall come to pass that whosoever shall believe on the Son of God, the same shall have everlasting life.
>
> 9 And behold, thus hath the Lord commanded me, by his angel, that I should come and tell this thing unto you; yea, he hath commanded that I should prophesy these things unto you; yea, he hath said unto me: Cry unto this people, repent and prepare the way of the Lord. (Helaman 14:2–9)

Prophecy Fulfilled

Unfortunately, many of the Nephites were just as stiff-necked as some of the Hebrews back in the Old World, and they did not believe in such teachings. But, true to prophecy, the signs came.

> 4 And it came to pass that in the commencement of the ninety and second year, behold, the prophecies of the prophets began to be fulfilled more fully; for there began to be greater signs and greater miracles wrought among the people.
>
> 5 But there were some who began to say that the time was past for the words to be fulfilled, which were spoken by Samuel, the Lamanite. . . .
>
> 9 Now it came to pass that there was a day set apart by the unbelievers, that all those who believed in those traditions should be put to death except the sign should come to pass, which had been given by Samuel the prophet.
>
> 10 Now it came to pass that when Nephi, the son of Nephi, saw this wickedness of his people, his heart was exceedingly sorrowful.
>
> 11 And it came to pass that he went out and bowed himself down upon the earth, and cried mightily to his God in behalf of his people, yea, those who were about to be destroyed because of their faith in the tradition of their fathers.
>
> 12 And it came to pass that he cried mightily unto the Lord all that day; and behold, the voice of the Lord came unto him, saying:
>
> 13 Lift up your head and be of good cheer; for behold, the time is at hand, and on this night shall the sign be given, and on the morrow come I into the world, to show unto the world that I will fulfil all that which I have caused to be spoken by the mouth of my holy prophets.
>
> 14 Behold, I come unto my own, to fulfil all things which I have made known unto the children of men from the foundation of the world, and to do the will, both of the Father and of the Son—of the Father because of me, and of the Son because of my flesh. And behold, the time is at hand, and this night shall the sign be given.
>
> 15 And it came to pass that the words which came unto Nephi were fulfilled, according as they had been spoken; for behold, at the going down of the sun there was no darkness; and the people began to be astonished because there was no darkness when the night came.
>
> 16 And there were many, who had not believed the words of the prophets, who fell to the earth and became as if they were dead, for

they knew that the great plan of destruction which they had laid for those who believed in the words of the prophets had been frustrated; for the sign which had been given was already at hand.

17 And they began to know that the Son of God must shortly appear; yea, in fine, all the people upon the face of the whole earth from the west to the east, both in the land north and in the land south, were so exceedingly astonished that they fell to the earth.

19 And it came to pass that there was no darkness in all that night, but it was as light as though it was mid-day. And it came to pass that the sun did rise in the morning again, according to its proper order; and they knew that it was the day that the Lord should be born, because of the sign which had been given.

20 And it had come to pass, yea, all things, every whit, according to the words of the prophets.

21 And it came to pass also that a new star did appear, according to the word. (3 Nephi 1:4–21)

Notes

1. For more information on the fascinating story of the Zarahline of kings see Phyllis Carol Olive, *The Lost Sheep of Ancient America: Bringing the Lands and People of the Book of Mormon to Life* (Springville, UT: Cedar Fort, Inc., 2015).
2. Phyllis Carol Olive, *The Lost Sheep of Ancient America: Bringing the Lands and People of the Book of Mormon to Life* (Springville, UT: Cedar Fort, Inc., 2015).
3. Cyrus Gordon, *Before Columbus: Links between the Old World and Ancient America* (Crown Pub, 1971), 51.
4. Gene Matlock, *India Once Ruled the Americas!* (Lincoln, NE: iUniverse, 2000), 7.
5. Ibid.
6. Ibid.

7. Ibid.
8. Ibid., 6–7.
9. Ibid., 7.
10. *Wikipedia*, s.v. "Hopi mythology," last modified March 9, 2017, en.wikipedia.org/wiki/Hopi_mythology.
11. Frank Waters, *Book of the Hopi* (New York: Penguin Books, 1977), 21.
12. "Dr. Fewkes and Masauwu," Edmund Nequatewa, *The South Corner of Time*, accessed March 23, 2017, parentseyes.arizona.edu/southcorner/hopi_drfewkes.html.
13. Hugh Nibley, *Teachings of the Book of Mormon*, lecture 60, in "The Ancient and the Academic: Hugh Nibley's Teaching, Dealings and Understanding of the Hopi," Jody Livingston, *Book of Mormon Archaeological Forum*, accessed March 15, 2017, www.bmaf.org/node/451.
14. "Hopis," Ellen French and Richard C. Hanes, *Countries and Their Cultures*, accessed March 23, 2017, www.everyculture.com/multi/Ha-La/Hopis.html.
15. Jerry Jackson, "Overcoming Illiteracy: God's Word and Lasting Fruit," *Lausanne World Pulse Archives*, no. 7, (2009), www.lausanneworldpulse.com/themedarticles-php/1164/07-2009.
16. Ojibwa, "Mormon Missionaries and the Hopi Indians," *Native American Netroots*, November 11, 2010, accessed March 23, 2017, nativeamericannetroots.net/diary/758.
17. "Are You Related to the Aztecs?: Uto-Aztecan Languages Spoken Throughout Mexico and the Western United States," John P. Schmal, *Traditions of Mexico*, accessed March 23, 2017, www.houstonculture.org/mexico/aztec.html.

6

The Time of Christ

Great destruction hit the promised land prior to the Savior's visit to His New World flock (a minor foreshadowing to the destruction that will hit the entire world at the time of His Second Coming). So many sun-worshiping tribes had filtered into northeastern America from the southeastern states (having sailed up the Mississippi by ship or traveled by land through the Cumberland Gap in Tennessee) that some of the Nephites living in New York became corrupted by their false philosophies and religions. Some Celtiberians (the Celtic tribes of Iberia) living in New England also moved west across Pennsylvania, West Virginia, Kentucky, Tennessee, and then into Ohio, bringing their sun-worshiping ways with them as well. Now, they too bordered the Nephites living in New York. Thus, it is no surprise that so many of the seed of Lehi, especially the Lamanites, fell in line with their corrupt philosophies. False Christs and prophets had appeared among the Nephites long before the time of Christ. Mormon writes,

> 15 And it came to pass that after there had been false Christs, and their mouths had been shut, and they punished according to their crimes;
>
> 16 And after there had been false prophets, and false preachers and teachers among the people, and all these having been punished according to their crimes. (Words of Mormon 1:15–16)

The Hopewell

As more and more people began to filter into Ohio (some from the southeastern states, some from Tennessee, and some from New York and lower Ontario), a new culture began to rise up between 100 and 50 BC. This new culture was called the Hopewell. In his research of the rise of the Hopewell mound building culture, the archaeologist Don Dragoo concluded that a privileged minority somehow came to dominate the area, and in time imposed their religion on the established tribes of Ohio and the surrounding areas.[1] Although the Nephites back in New York show evidence of *non-compliance* with the perverted philosophies and traditions of the Hopewell, the changes that were sweeping through the entire region in the first century before Christ understandably affected those in Zarahemla as well. Various anti-Christs, such as Nehor, filtered into both the land of Zarahemla and the land of Nephi. The more wicked part of the Lamanites were after the order of Nehor (see Alma 24:28–29.) The anti-Christ was most likely affiliated with the Druidic priesthood of the Celtic tribes among them because he brought an entirely different religious order with him that in many ways resembled the Druidic order of Ireland. One of the most damning notions taught by Nehor was a fallacious principle practiced by the Druids, that there was no need for repentance. Of the Druids we learn that the "Irish 'Der,' a Druid, is the absolver and remitter of sins."[2]

The Book of Mormon tells us a bit more about those who followed the profession of Nehor, such as those living in the great city of Ammonihah who continually rejected the missionary efforts of Alma and his companions. We read, "But as to the people that were in the land of Ammonihah, they yet remained a hard-hearted and a stiffnecked people; and they repented not of their sins, ascribing all the power of Alma and Amulek to the devil; for they were of the profession of Nehor, and did not believe in the repentance of their sins" (Alma 15:15).

The Druids also believed in reincarnation, and that "every soul, however frequent its relapses, will ultimately attain the proper end of its existence—reunion with God."[3] Nehor taught the Nephites a similar philosophy, "And he also testified unto the people that all mankind should be saved at the last day, and that they need not fear nor tremble, but that they might lift up their heads and rejoice; for the Lord had created all men, and had also redeemed all men; and, in the end, all men should have eternal life" (Alma 1:4).

There was so much corruption spreading through the land in the first century before Christ that the land had to be cleansed because such counterfeit philosophies were not compatible with the doctrines of Christ and His great plan of happiness. Many of the Lamanites had already become corrupted by such satanic philosophies, with many of the Nephites even moving south to join them. Thus, it becomes more and more obvious why the Lord had to cleanse the land; the Savior had a message for His New World flock that was far different from the counterfeit philosophies that were now permeating the region.

Three Days of Darkness

According to the Bible, the sun refused to shine for three full hours at the time of the Savior's death, a phenomenon that many attribute to an eclipse of the sun. "Now from the sixth hour there was darkness over all the land unto the ninth hour" (Matthew 27:45). Whatever the cause of the darkness, it can hardly be doubted that the sun hid her face for a time.

> 20 And it came to pass that there was thick darkness upon all the face of the land, insomuch that the inhabitants thereof who had not fallen could feel the vapor of darkness;
>
> 21 And there could be no light, because of the darkness, neither candles, neither torches; neither could there be fire kindled with their fine and exceedingly dry wood, so that there could not be any light at all. (3 Nephi 8:20–21)

Something big was happening, including an earthquake. While modern scientific evidence is lacking, the powerful earthquake that hit the Book of Mormon territory in the American northeast could well have caused many volcanoes along the rim of the Atlantic to erupt, including those in Iceland; Labrador, Canada; Maine; New Hampshire; and perhaps even in one of the five calderas in the super volcano just to the north of New York in lower Canada. These volcanic eruptions would have caused tempests, lightning, fire from heaven, and even vapors of darkness. The Indians still speak of fire-mountains in Labrador, which is a sure indication that they were active much longer than modern scientific researchers suppose. It was Nephi who noticed the connection between the three days of darkness that the Nephites would experience and the three days of palpable darkness that the Lord inflicted upon the Egyptians in His ongoing efforts to facilitate the Hebrews' release after four hundred years of bondage to Pharaoh,

> 21 And the Lord said unto Moses, Stretch out thine hand toward heaven, that there may be darkness over the land of Egypt, even darkness which may be felt.
>
> 22 And Moses stretched forth his hand toward heaven; and there was a thick darkness in all the land of Egypt three days. (Exodus 10:21–22)

Nephi explains,

> And the God of our fathers, who were led out of Egypt, out of bondage, and also were preserved in the wilderness by him, yea, the God of Abraham, and of Isaac, and the God of Jacob, yieldeth himself, according to the words of the angel, as a man, into the hands of wicked men, to be lifted up, according to the words of Zenock, and to be crucified, according to the words of Neum, and to be buried in a sepulchre, according to the words of Zenos, which he spake concerning *the three days of darkness*, which should be a sign given of his death unto those who should inhabit the isles of the sea, more especially given unto those who are of the house of Israel. (1 Nephi 19:10; emphasis added)

The Great Destruction

The Lamanite prophet Samuel prophesied about the terrible destruction that would accompany the Savior's death. He said,

> 20 But behold, as I said unto you concerning another sign, a sign of his death, behold, in that day that he shall suffer death the sun shall be darkened and refuse to give his light unto you; and also the moon and the stars; and there shall be no light upon the face of this land, even from the time that he shall suffer death, for the space of three days, to the time that he shall rise again from the dead. . . .
>
> 26 And behold, thus hath the angel spoken unto me; for he said unto me that there should be thunderings and lightnings for the space of many hours.
>
> 27 And he said unto me that while the thunder and the lightning lasted, and the tempest, that these things should be, and that darkness

should cover the face of the whole earth for the space of three days. (Helaman 14:20, 26–27)

This prophecy stuck in the minds of the Nephites throughout the years until the time came when they witnessed its fulfillment. In recapping those terrible events noted in 3 Nephi 8:3–23, we learn that "in the thirty and fourth year, in the first month, on the fourth day of the month, there arose a great storm, such an one as never had been known in all the land" (verse 5). It was accompanied by a "great and terrible tempest" (verse 6) with thunder so loud, it shook the whole earth, accompanied by unbelievable lightening. Whole cities were destroyed as the undulated earth carried the land up over buildings and created new mountains, while other cities slipped from their moorings and sank beneath neighboring seas, drowning all their inhabitants. Some people were even carried away in whirlwinds, and where they ended up no one knows.

> 17 And thus the face of the whole earth became deformed, because of the tempests, and the thunderings, and the lightnings, and the quaking of the earth. . . .
>
> 19 For behold, they did last for about the space of three hours . . . and then behold, there was darkness upon the face of the land.
>
> 20 And it came to pass that there was thick darkness upon all the face of the land, insomuch that the inhabitants thereof who had not fallen could feel the vapor of darkness;
>
> 21 And there could be no light, because of the darkness, neither candles, neither torches; neither could there be fire kindled with their fine and exceedingly dry wood, so that there could not be any light at all;
>
> 22 And there was not any light seen, neither fire, nor glimmer, neither the sun, nor the moon, nor the stars, for so great were the mists of darkness which were upon the face of the land.
>
> 23 And it came to pass that it *did last for the space of three days that there was no light seen*; and there was great mourning and howling and weeping among all the people continually; yea, great were the groanings of the people, because of the darkness and the great destruction which had come upon them (3 Nephi 8:17, 19–23; emphasis added).

There was darkness and an earthquake reported in Mexico as well. H. H. Bancroft explains, "One hundred and sixteen years after this regulation or invention of the Toltec calendar, 'the sun and moon were eclipsed, the earth shook, and the rocks were rent asunder, and many other things and signs happened, though there was no loss of life. This was in the year Ce Calli, which, the chronology being reduced to our systems, proves to be the same date when Christ our Lord suffered' (AD 33)."[4]

The fact that no deaths were reported in Mexico makes it clear that the major area of destruction described in the Book of Mormon took place far from the Mexican heartland. The scriptures say that untold numbers were destroyed in Nephite territory at the time of the Savior's death, chiefly the more wicked among them, but the death toll must have been horrendous.

The Visit of Jesus Christ

Once the sun was seen in the skies again, and the tempests and earthquakes had ceased, the Nephites (and the righteous Lamanites) who survived the destruction enjoyed a time of unbelievable wonder—the risen Lord appeared to them in the flesh. The Savior's appearance to His faithful flock near the temple in Bountiful was so glorious that words alone cannot express the grandeur of that occasion. It was the Lord God Omnipotent Himself who introduced His Son, Jesus Christ. His voice was so soft that the crowds could barely hear it the first time around, or even the second. But once God had the full attention of the crowd gathered at the temple, He introduced His beloved Son, saying, "*Behold my Beloved Son, in whom I am well pleased, in whom I have glorified my name—hear ye him*" (3 Nephi 11:7).

The first thing the resurrected Lord said upon greeting the Nephites in Bountiful was,

> 10 Behold, I am Jesus Christ, whom the prophets testified shall come into the world.
>
> 11 And behold, I am the light and the life of the world; and I have drunk out of that bitter cup which the Father hath given me, and have glorified the Father in taking upon me the sins of the world, in the which I have suffered the will of the Father in all things from the beginning. (3 Nephi 11:8–11)

The name Jesus Christ is the name that has been an integral part of His identity from the beginning of time and will continue to be throughout the eternities. But of equal importance, it will be by *His name* and by none other that salvation comes to the children of man (see Mosiah 3:17). To leave no questions in their minds that He was the true Messiah, He asked the crowd congregated at the temple to feel the nail prints in His hands and feet and to thrust their hands into the wound in His side. The scriptures relate, "And it came to pass that the multitude went forth, and thrust their hands into his side, and did feel the prints of the nails in his hands and in his feet; and this they did do, going forth one by one until they had all gone forth, and did see with their eyes and did feel with their hands, and did know of a surety and did bear record, that it was he, of whom it was written by the prophets, that should come (3 Nephi 11:15).

The Lord then blessed them, and organized His church among them.

> 16 The eye hath never seen, neither hath the ear heard, before, so great and marvelous things as we saw and heard Jesus speak unto the Father;
>
> 17 And no tongue can speak, neither can there be written by any man, neither can the hearts of men conceive so great and marvelous things as we both saw and heard Jesus speak; and no one can conceive of the joy which filled our souls at the time we heard him pray for us unto the Father. . . .
>
> 21 And he took their little children, one by one, and blessed them, and prayed unto the Father for them. (3 Nephi 17:16–17, 21)

The scriptures say He chose twelve disciples from among the Nephites and instructed them in every aspect of religious government. He even provided the name whereby His church should be known: His name, for it is His church, and thus should be named after Him, and no one else! The Lord gave them instructions on daily living (similar to the Beatitudes), and commanded them to baptize in His name—all except little children, who were exempt from that ordinance until the age of accountability because they are innocent and are naturally saved by virtue of His Atonement. (For details of the Savior's visit to the New World, see 3 Nephi 11–27).

The Gospel of Christ

The Lord did more than just heal the Nephites and teach them to pray and how to live in peace with one another. He taught them of His Atonement, and what they needed to do to wash themselves clean of sin so that they would be worthy to enter heaven. He said:

> 19 And no unclean thing can enter into his kingdom; therefore nothing entereth into his rest save it be those who have washed their garments in my blood, because of their faith, and the repentance of all their sins, and their faithfulness unto the end.
>
> 20 Now this is the commandment: Repent, all ye ends of the earth, and come unto me and be baptized in my name, that ye may be sanctified by the reception of the Holy Ghost, that ye may stand spotless before me at the last day.
>
> 21 Verily, verily, I say unto you, this is my gospel; and ye know the things that ye must do in my church; for the works which ye have seen me do that shall ye also do; for that which ye have seen me do even that shall ye do;
>
> 22 Therefore, if ye do these things blessed are ye, for ye shall be lifted up at the last day. (3 Nephi 27:19–22)

The Lord Prophesied of the Future

Before Jesus departed from the Nephites to visit others of His scattered flock, He prophesied of the future. He told of the rise of a free people in the land of promise (the Gentiles) and of the coming forth of the Book of Mormon, which would inaugurate the Restoration of the gospel and signal the gathering of Israel. He spoke of a time when the Lamanites would be among the Gentiles like a lion among the sheep (see 3 Nephi 20:16), and of the ultimate rise of the New Jerusalem (see 3 Nephi 20:22). He foretold of the time when the Lamanites would be restored to their rightful lands of inheritance (see 3 Nephi 29:1), and of their ultimate return to the faith of their fathers. He then spoke of a time when the righteous would be gathered out from among the wicked (see 3 Nephi 20:18) and when the Jerusalem of old would once again be filled with His own people, the Jews (3 Nephi 20:46).

The Twelve Disciples

Before the Lord departed, He ordained twelve disciples to carry His message to the Nephites, bring them to repentance, baptize them, and give them the Holy Ghost because Christ was not destined to be among them for very long. The names of the twelve disciples that the Lord ordained are given in the Book of Mormon: Nephi, Timothy, Jonas, Mathoni, Mathonihah, Kumen, Kumenonhi, Jeremiah, Shemnon, Jonas, Zedekiah, and Isaiah. Three of these disciples (like John the Beloved) were blessed by the Lord to tarry until His Second Coming. All of them took their commission seriously and went out among their brethren to preach the gospel of Christ. "And it came to pass that thus they did go forth among all the people of Nephi, and did preach the gospel of Christ unto all people upon the face of the land; and they were converted unto the Lord, and were united unto the church of Christ, and thus the people of that generation were blessed, according to the word of Jesus" (3 Nephi 28:23).

Everything done by these valiant servants of God was done in the *name of Jesus.* "And there were great and marvelous works wrought by the disciples of Jesus, insomuch that they did heal the sick, and raise the dead, and cause the lame to walk, and the blind to receive their sight, and the deaf to hear; and all manner of miracles did they work among the children of men; *and in nothing did they work miracles save it were in the name of Jesus*" (4 Nephi 1:5; emphasis added).

In *The Works of Hubert Howe Bancroft* (a book about the native races of America), we find references to men mysteriously appearing and disappearing from one group of astonished people or another throughout the hemisphere around the time of Christ. These appearances may well speak of a visit by the Savior, but most were likely not. Most were likely visitations by one of the Lord's appointed servants. For example, Nephi, the son of Helaman, was given the sealing powers because of his righteousness and was then carried by the Spirit from congregation to congregation to preach of God even before the Savior's visit to the Nephites (see Helaman 10:14–17).

There is also the interesting tale of "Bochica, a white man with a beard, [who] appeared to the Mozca Indians in the plains of Bogata. [He] taught them how to build and to sow, formed them into communities, gave an outlet to the waters of the great lake, and, having settled the government civil and ecclesiastical, retired into a monastic state of penitence for two thousand years."[5] Since the three Nephites had no need for repentance when they began their long mission, having been given the powers to live until the Savior's return, the fact that he stayed among them for two thousand years makes it clear that this was not the Savior, who had long since returned to His Father in Heaven. But who can say that others of the Lord's scattered flock weren't given powers of longevity as well?

The Lord also warned His flock (both in the Old and New World) of false Christs and prophets, saying,

> 24 For there shall arise false Christs, and false prophets, and shall shew great signs and wonders; insomuch that, if it were possible, they shall deceive the very elect.
>
> 25 Behold, I have told you before.
>
> 26 Wherefore if they shall say unto you, Behold, he is in the desert; go not forth: behold, he is in the secret chambers; believe it not. (Matthew 24:24–26; see also Words of Mormon 1:15)

Conversion of the Lamanites

While the twelve Apostles of Christ in the Old World were commissioned to preach throughout the entire world, the twelve Nephite disciples were commissioned to preach particularly among those in America. Thus, they had a great mission ahead of them. One of their greatest challenges was teaching the Lamanites. Yet, as the twelve disciples went out among the Nephites to preach and teach the doctrines of Christ, huge numbers of the Lamanites were also converted because only the more righteous among them had survived the great destruction. Thus, within just a few years (AD 36), the people were all converted to the Lord, both the Nephites and the Lamanites:

> 1 And it came to pass that the thirty and fourth year passed away, and also the thirty and fifth, and behold the disciples of Jesus had formed a church of Christ in all the lands round about. And as many as did come unto them, and did truly repent of their sins, were baptized in the name of Jesus; and they did also receive the Holy Ghost.
>
> 2 And it came to pass in the thirty and sixth year, the people were all converted unto the Lord, upon all the face of the land, both Nephites

> and Lamanites, and there were no contentions and disputations among them, and every man did deal justly one with another. (4 Nephi 1:1–2)

The Golden Age of Peace

The episode of the Savior's visit to the faithful in Bountiful was itself such a glorious experience that the people enjoyed a time of peace. With the destruction of the more wicked, the Nephites could now mingle freely with the Lamanites, for all had been converted to the gospel of Christ.

> 17 There were no robbers, nor murderers, neither were there Lamanites, nor any manner of -ites; but they were in one, the children of Christ, and heirs to the kingdom of God.
>
> 18 And how blessed were they! For the Lord did bless them in all their doings; yea, even they were blessed and prospered until an hundred and ten years had passed away; and the first generation from Christ had passed away, and there was no contention in all the land. (4 Nephi 1:17–18)

During this golden age of peace, the trade network of the Hopewell reached its climax, with their elaborate exchange network now reaching nearly continental proportions. They were capable of amassing resources from the Rocky Mountains to the Appalachians, and across the mountains to the Atlantic, and from the Great Lakes to the Gulf of Mexico. This was a glorious time to live in the promised land, for peace prevailed in the land for the next two hundred years—a small precursor to the time of peace that the Savior will usher in at the end of the world and at the beginning of His great millennial reign.

> 14 And it came to pass that the seventy and first year passed away, and also the seventy and second year, yea, and in fine, till the seventy and ninth year had passed away; yea, even an hundred years had passed away, and the disciples of Jesus, whom he had chosen, had all gone to the paradise of God, save it were the three who should tarry; and there were other disciples ordained in their stead; and also many of that generation had passed away.
>
> 15 And it came to pass that there was no contention in the land, because of the love of God which did dwell in the hearts of the people.
>
> 16 And there were no envyings, nor strifes, nor tumults, nor whoredoms, nor lyings, nor murders, nor any manner of lasciviousness;

and surely there could not be a happier people among all the people who had been created by the hand of God.

17 There were no robbers, nor murderers, neither were there Lamanites, nor any manner of -ites; but they were in one, the children of Christ, and heirs to the kingdom of God.

18 And how blessed were they! For the Lord did bless them in all their doings; yea, even they were blessed and prospered until an hundred and ten years had passed away; and the first generation from Christ had passed away, and there was no contention in all the land. (4 Nephi 1:14–18)

The Twelve Apostles Back in the Old World

While the missionary excursions of the Three Nephites and others of the Lord's New World disciples have not yet been revealed, we do have reports of the various missions of the twelve Apostles in the Old World being fulfilled. Various accounts including George F. Jowett, in his impressive book, *The Drama of the Lost Disciples*, include Andrew going to Macedonia, Greece, Scythia, Asia Minor, and Russia. Bartholomew went mainly to India and Armenia. The Apostle James preached in Persia and Spain. John traveled to Palestine and Asia Minor; Matthew to Egypt and Ethiopia; Philip to France, southern Russia, and Asia Minor; Peter to Pontius, Galatia, Bithynia, Cappadocia, and Asia; and Simon to Egypt, Mauritania, Africa, Libya, and Britain. Thomas preached in India and to the Parthians, the Medes, and the Persians, with some writers claiming he also made it to China and America. Philip is said to have consecrated Joseph of Arimathea to the work while he was in Gaul (modern-day France). He then went on to preach of Christ in England.[6] (Lazarus, who Jesus raised from the dead, also became a missionary and went west—where some of the disciples met from time to time, particularly in France and England.)

Celtic Christianity

While conversions in America appear to be widespread, many of those who formerly espoused the old pagan traditions of sun and serpent worship simply merged the new with the old. Even some of the Celtic tribes merged their old philosophies with the new into a form of Celtic-Christianity: the mixing of both religions into one because they believed that it made no difference whether they believed in one supreme god or a multitude of gods. This, of course, is just one more fallacious lie perpetuated by the devil in his efforts to thwart the spread of Christianity. In my earlier work, *The Lost Empires and Vanished Races of the Book of Mormon*, I bring this issue into focus with archaeological evidence that shows that many of the tribes of the American southeast combined the new religion of Christ with their old sun-worshiping ways. Evidence indicates that those in Mexico also succumbed to the tradition of merging Christianity with their old pagan practices of sun and serpent worship.

Christ's Mission Exclusive to the House of Israel

So many legends about pale gods or prophets have been discovered in the Americas that we cannot help but believe that some may have been speaking of a legitimate visitation of the Savior. However, caution is needed here, for only those of Israelite blood would have enjoyed such a visit. It would not have been just any group of Israelites either, but of those not steeped in sun worship or other sinful traditions. The risen Lord did not even visit all the outlying regions around Jerusalem when He appeared to His twelve Apostles after His death and Resurrection. While there were Israelites living in nearby Samaria, the Samaritans were of mixed blood, and the Lord's mission was exclusively to the house of Israel, leaving those of other bloodlines to be converted by the Spirit and by His various Apostles. Thus, it stands to reason that only those of Israelite blood would have enjoyed a visitation by the risen Lord in the New World as well. Even the pure-blooded Nephites in Bountiful had to be weeded out. Only the more righteous were favored to a visit by the risen Lord, with those of mixed blood hearing the glad news of the gospel through His many walking prophets.

The Lord Himself revealed to the Nephites that His mission was exclusively to the house of Israel. He said,

> 12 Ye are my disciples; and ye are a light unto this people, who are a remnant of the house of Joseph.
>
> 13 And behold, this is the land of your inheritance; and the Father hath given it unto you.
>
> 14 And not at any time hath the Father given me commandment that I should tell it unto your brethren at Jerusalem.

15 Neither at any time hath the Father given me commandment that I should tell unto them concerning the other tribes of the house of Israel, whom the Father hath led away out of the land.

16 This much did the Father command me, that I should tell unto them:

17 That other sheep I have which are not of this fold; them also I must bring, and they shall hear my voice; and there shall be one fold, and one shepherd.

18 And now, because of stiffneckedness and unbelief they understood not my word; therefore I was commanded to say no more of the Father concerning this thing unto them.

19 But, verily, I say unto you that the Father hath commanded me, and I tell it unto you, that ye were separated from among them because of their iniquity; therefore it is because of their iniquity that they know not of you.

20 And verily, I say unto you again that the other tribes hath the Father separated from them; and it is because of their iniquity that they know not of them.

21 And verily I say unto you, that ye are they of whom I said: Other sheep I have which are not of this fold; them also I must bring, and they shall hear my voice; and there shall be one fold, and one shepherd.

22 And they understood me not, for they supposed it had been the Gentiles; for they understood not that the Gentiles should be converted through their preaching.

23 And they understood me not that I said they shall hear my voice; and they understood me not that the Gentiles should not at any time hear my voice—that I should not manifest myself unto them save it were by the Holy Ghost.

24 But behold, ye have both heard my voice, and seen me; and ye are my sheep, and ye are numbered among those whom the Father hath given me. (3 Nephi 15:12–24)

Only Worthy Israel Would Be Privileged to See the Savior

Not only was the Lord mindful of the lineage of those He visited, but He was mindful of their worthiness as well. No visit would have been made atop the great pyramid temples that reeked with the blood of human sacrifice, or encased the dead of their kings and nobles (a common tradition throughout the Americas). Even some of the Nephites had succumbed to such traditions once they began to mingle with the Hopewell mound builders of the Ohio and Mississippi River valleys. Yet, the righteous who kept themselves clean from such ungodliness would not be disappointed. After the great destruction that cleansed the land of the wicked, the Lord slowly descended upon the scene of Nephites gathered together at the temple in Bountiful. This temple was not a great pyramid structure like the pagan tribes built, but more like the temple of Solomon. While not altogether spotless, only the more righteous Nephites would be privileged to greet the Savior, a fact they learned from the Lord Himself, who said,

> 12 And many great destructions have I caused to come upon this land, and upon this people, because of their wickedness and their abominations.
>
> 13 O all ye that are spared because ye were more righteous than they, will ye not now return unto me, and repent of your sins, and be converted, that I may heal you?
>
> 14 Yea, verily I say unto you, if ye will come unto me ye shall have eternal life. Behold, mine arm of mercy is extended towards you, and whosoever will come, him will I receive; and blessed are those who come unto me.
>
> 15 Behold, I am Jesus Christ the Son of God. I created the heavens and the earth, and all things that in them are. I was with the Father from the beginning. I am in the Father, and the Father in me; and in me hath the Father glorified his name. (3 Nephi 9:12–22)

The Latter-Day Conversion of the Lamanites

While the Lamanites continued to believe in the Great Spirit throughout the centuries, future conversions would come in the latter days, as prophesied by the Savior. Starting in 1883–84, a large number of the Catawba branch of the Sioux (close brothers of the Iroquois—those most closely related to the Lamanite branch of the Nephites), joined The Church of Jesus Christ of Latter-day Saints. Some Catawba migrated west with the Saints to Colorado.[7] Yet, much is left to be done before all the descendants of Lehi are received back into the fold of Christ. This is a prophecy yet to be fulfilled.

Notes

1. Don W. Dragoo in Joseph R. Caldwell and Robert L. Hall, eds., *Hopewellian Studies* (Springfield, IL: Illinois State Museum, 1970), 25.
2. E. O. Gordon, *Prehistoric London: Its Mounds and Circles*, 4th ed. (London: Covenant Publishing, 1946), 23.
3. Ibid.
4. Hubert Howe Bancroft, *The Works of Hubert Howe Bancroft: The Native Races* (San Francisco: A. L. Bancroft and Company, 1883), 5:210.
5. Ibid., 3:33.
6. George F. Jowett, *The Drama of the Lost Disciples* (Covenant Publishing, 2001), 69.
7. *Wikipedia*, s.v. "Catawba people," last modified January 29, 2017, en.wikipedia.org/wiki/Catawba_people.

7

The Pale Prophet Quetzalcoatl

There are two legends that persist in Mexico and Central America, one of which speaks of a culture hero and high priest named Quetzalcoatl, and the other speaks of a pale prophet known by the names of both Kate-Zahl and Quetzal. Many believe Quetzalcoatl and Kate-Zahl, or Quetzal, to be the same person, but were they, and do either refer to the Savior? Quetzalcoatl (a name derived from both the Quetzal bird and the serpent), was the name given to the supreme god of all the Nahuatl tribes, including the Nahuas, Toltecs, and the wilder Chichimec tribes and the later Aztecs. Others tribes, such as the Maya, also venerated him, but referred to him as the Plumed, or Feathered Serpent. They also referred to him as Q'uq'umatz or Kukulcan—a name they often gave their culture heroes, much like the Nahuas referred to their culture heroes as Quetzalcoatl. Unfortunately, such stories have led some to suppose that these legends were speaking of a visit by the Savior Himself, rather than a mortal man who was given the name Quetzalcoatl as a title of his office as high priest over his people.

According to the early historian Torquemada, the name Quetzalcoatl in the Mexican annals means "snake that has plumage."[1] The worship of the Feathered Serpent was said to have begun in Mexico around the first century (sometime before or after the time of Christ), which left some to suppose that they might be speaking of the Savior's visit to the Americas because the Book of Mormon clearly documents the wondrous visit of the Savior to His New World flock shortly after His death and Resurrection. As one legend goes, "Several years after the great eclipse, in a year that was indicated with the hieroglyph of the Reed in the number one (which according to the tables seems to have been the year 63 of Jesus Christ), a white and bearded man of good stature came to these regions through the northern part, dressed in an ankle-length tunic adorned with red crosses, barefoot, his head uncovered, and a staff in his hand, whom some call Quetzalcoatl, others Cocolcan and others Hueman."[2]

This holy man is said to have taught them to overcome their passions and to hate vice and love virtue. It is said that he also instituted a forty-day fast, and taught them to mortify, or humble, themselves by the shedding of their own blood in penance for their sins. He introduced the cross and promised that by using that sign that they would be assured of rain, prosperity, health, and just about anything else they wanted or needed.[3]

Quetzalcoatl Arrives in America

Brasseur de Bourbourg, one of the more respected investigators of the early history of ancient Mexico, said,

> Previous to the history of the Toltec domination in Mexico, we notice in the annals of the country two facts of great importance, but equally obscure in their details: first, the tradition concerning the landing of a foreign race, conducted by an illustrious personage, who came from an eastern country; and second, the existence of an ancient empire known as Huehue-Tlapalan, from which the Toltecs or Nahuas came to Mexico, in consequence of a revolution or invasion, and from which they had a long and toilsome migration to the Aztec plateau.[4]

As to who brought this illustrious man across the sea to America, he was likely brought to the country by the Phoenicians, many of which were Israelites of the tribe of Dan who became some of the greatest seafaring men of their day. Of Quetzalcoatl's subsequent arrival in Mexico, Bourbourg said,

> Certain people came from the north. . . . These were men of good carriage, well-dressed in long robes of black linen, open in front, and without capes, cut low at the neck, with short sleeves that did not come to the elbow. . . . They brought with them as their chief and head a personage called Quetzalcoatl, a fair and ruddy complexioned man,

> with a long beard. . . . These followers of Quetzalcoatl were men of great knowledge and cunning artists in all kinds of fine work.[5]

Men Made into Gods

Unfortunately, the religion in Mexico was a compound of spiritualism and gross idolatry at that time and for a long time after. While the locals continued to believe in a supreme being (which they generally took to be the sun), they added to their worship a number of other deities as well: two thousand in all, with one for nearly everything imaginable.[6] Even so, they revered their supreme being and believed they owed him tribute in the way of sacrifice, sometimes human. Thus, with the introduction of Christianity, human sacrifice had to be done away with. Quetzalcoatl was one of the first to insist on that change, which earned him the status of a god. In fact, Quetzalcoatl was considered the supreme lord of the land, much as the Pope is regarded as the head pontiff in the Catholic Church. While Torquemada affirms Quetzalcoatl's status as a god, he gives Quetzalcoatl a far different description than one might expect when describing Jesus Christ. He said, "This god Quetzalcoatl was very celebrated among the people of the city of Cholula. . . . It is said of Quetzalcoatl that he was a white man, large-bodied, broad-browed, great-eyed, with long black hair, and a beard heavy and rounded. He was a great artificer, and very ingenious. He taught many mechanical arts."[7]

Whatever controversy surrounds Quetzalcoatl, all the accounts agree that he was venerable, just, and holy. He taught by precept and example the paths of virtue in all the Nahua cities, particularly in Cholula. During his life there, he is said to have worn "for the sake of modesty, garments that reached down to [his] feet with a blanket over all, sown with red crosses."[8] The ruling clerics during the rule of Quetzalcoatl all lived very austere lives. They mortified the flesh in penance, often by self-flogging, in imitation of Quetzalcoatl, their patron deity.[9] However, Christ did not mortify His flesh in penance because He was perfect through and through—an important factor leading any discussion away from Quetzalcoatl actually being Christ, because Christ asked only for a broken heart and a contrite spirit in penance for sin because He had already atoned for the sins of the world: "And behold, I have given you the law and the commandments of my Father, that ye shall believe in me, and that ye shall repent of your sins, and come unto me with a broken heart and a contrite spirit. Behold, ye have the commandments before you, and the law is fulfilled" (3 Nephi 12:19).

The Pale Prophet

All of the ruling high priests in Mexico were given the title "Quetzalcoatl" over a span of a thousand years (all of which are recognized as mortal men). Yet, still another figure shows up on the scene which has grabbed the attention of many because he too showed up sometime around the time of Christ. In her popular book, *He Walked the Americas*, L. Taylor Hansen gathered together legends of a visit by a pale, bearded prophet known in Mexico as Quetzal or Kate-Zahl, who legends say walked the Americas. His suggested arrival around the time of Christ, (some say AD 63) left those who were reading the marvelous stories of this pious man thinking that they must surely be tales of the Savior's visit to New World flock shortly after His death and Resurrection. Yet, there are too many inconsistencies about the Pale Prophet to suppose that they were speaking about Jesus. One of the greatest inconsistencies is his refusal to give anyone his name. Although the Pale Prophet referred to God as "My Father," he had no interest in his own name at all. "He asked each tribe to name Him, for to Him names meant nothing."[10] Thus he was known by a variety of strange sounding names, each one different from the last. While it is not necessary that the name of a prophet or missionary be known, far too many people equate this illustrious man with the Savior whose name is and always has been the name by which mankind is saved. Rather than tell the Nephites they could call him anything they like, the first thing the Savior did when He appeared to the righteous Nephites was to announce His godhood:

> 10 Behold, I am Jesus Christ, whom the prophets testified shall come into the world.
>
> 11 And behold, I am the light and the life of the world; and I have drunk out of that bitter cup which the Father hath given me, and have glorified the Father in taking upon me the sins of the world, in the which I have suffered the will of the Father in all things from the beginning.

> 12 And it came to pass that when Jesus had spoken these words the whole multitude fell to the earth; for they remembered that it had been prophesied among them that Christ should show himself unto them after his ascension into heaven. (3 Nephi 11:10–12)

Not only is His name important in identifying Him, but it is also through His name that all holy ordinances are to be done. Even the Church was to be called by His sacred name:

> 6 And whoso taketh upon him *my name*, and endureth to the end, the same shall be saved at the last day.
>
> 7 Therefore, whatsoever ye shall do, ye shall do it *in my name*; therefore ye shall call the church in my name; and ye shall call upon the Father *in my name* that he will bless the church for my sake.
>
> 8 And how be it my church save it be called *in my name*? For if a church be called in Moses' name then it be Moses' church; or if it be called in the name of a man then it be the church of a man; but if it be called *in my name* then it is my church, if it so be that they are built upon my gospel.
>
> 9 Verily I say unto you, that ye are built upon my gospel; therefore ye shall call whatsoever things ye do call, *in my name*; therefore if ye call upon the Father, for the church, if it be in *my name* the Father will hear you. (3 Nephi 27:6–9; emphasis added)

Every ordinance performed by the disciples of Christ was to be done in the name of Jesus.

In 4 Nephi it says, "And there were great and marvelous works wrought by the disciples of Jesus, insomuch that they did heal the sick, and raise the dead, and cause the lame to walk, and the blind to receive their sight, and the deaf to hear; and all manner of miracles did they work among the children of men; and in nothing did they work miracles save it were *in the name of Jesus*" (4 Nephi 1:5; emphasis added).

And after this manner shall ye baptize *in my name*; for behold, verily I say unto you, that the Father, and the Son, and the Holy Ghost are one; and I am in the Father, and the Father in me, and the Father and I are one. (3 Nephi 11:27; emphasis added).

The Savior's Visit Was to the Righteous

Another interesting issue is the fact that the Pale Prophet is said to have visited both the righteous and the wicked, chastising those who indulged in human sacrifice, and miraculously defeating those who raised their swords against him. Yet, according to the Book of Mormon, the Savior did not come to the more wicked part of the Nephites. The terrible destruction that hit the Book of Mormon territory before the Savior descended out of heaven cleansed the land of the more wicked part of the people, leaving only the more righteous to greet the risen Lord. The mere fact that the Pale Prophet went in among the black-robed sacrificing priests in various regions is indication enough that this was not the Savior.

A Possible Identification

While some still cling to the notion that the culture hero Quetzalcoatl was the Savior, others believe he was the apostle Saint Thomas. Others suggest a possible tie to the Essenes, each of which will be addressed in the following pages. A possible clue to his identity might be tied in some way to the secret signs and handshakes the Pale Prophet gave to many of those he visited. These signs appear to be tied to the traditions of freemasonry, where the name of Jesus was never spoken in order to prevent offending those of different religions. This is the same diabolical tactic the devil is using today to take the name of Jesus out of every aspect of our lives.

Masonry

"Masons require one to believe in God to be a member, but the candidate is never required to say *what* god he believes in—'Masonry . . . requires merely that you believe in some deity, *give him what name you will . . . any god will do* [emphasis added], so he is your god.' "[11]

The Masons trace their organization's origin back to Solomon's temple. In the beginning, all Masonic lodges were consecrated to the Great Architect of the Universe and dedicated to King Solomon. Both John the Baptist and the Apostle John were said to be Masons. Even Saint Thomas had a connection. The symbol given to Saint Thomas is the "builder's square"—the most prominent symbol of Freemasonry. It is said that he built a palace for King Guduphara in India because the king wanted an architect for his own temple from among the people who had built the famous temple of King Solomon. From the Saint Thomas the Apostle Catholic Church, we learn that while Saint Thomas was in India, he became the patron saint of the blind as well as all craftsmen, such as architects, carpenters, and masons, and also of all geometricians and theologians.[12] While the Apostle Thomas is best known as "doubting Thomas," he nevertheless went to preach in Parthia, Persia, and India where he ultimately planted Christianity over a wide area.

Cultural Traits of the Saint Thomas Christians

The Saint Thomas Christians of India were ultimately made the legal patrons and supervisors of all carpenters, metal smelters, blacksmiths, goldsmiths, and barbers.[13] They were also known as astronomers and astrologists. They were adept in magic and esoteric healing—cultural traits that followed them all thoughout India, particularly in the south. These were the very same cultural traits brought to the Americas by the Pale Prophet. It is said that before his martyrdom at Mylapore in AD 72, Saint Thomas had converted 6,850 Brahmans, 2,800 Kshatriyas, 3,750 Vaishiyas, and 4,250 Shudras.[14]

Quetzalcoatl Seen as Saint Thomas

The Spanish Padres were convinced that Quetzalcoatl was Saint Thomas the apostle—a man who came to plant the cross and prepare the way for Christianity—because they knew he had gone to preach beyond the Ganges, the most sacred river of the Hindus. It is interesting to note that "snake" refers to the high status of snakes or (*nagas*) in Hindu mythology—with Quetzalcoatl's identity as a snake with plumage also fitting to one arriving from India. The Padres were so sure of this that they even created a statue of Saint Thomas in the village of Magdalena in central Mexico in his memory.[15]

> There were many reasons that Saint Thomas was assumed to be the Aztec's cultural hero Quetzalcoatl, not all reasons based on historical fact behind the story. The story of Saint Thomas as the missionary did not originally include the Americas. Originally, Saint Thomas was the missionary to the Indies and China, and according to legend and accounts from missionaries who visited China in later years who heard of his visits, he retired in the Indies. Yet as the age of discovery had dawned, and the world's geography was being remapped, it became apparent to the Franciscan missionaries that what had previously been referred to as the East where Saint Thomas had settled may actually have been the West (namely, Mexico and the Yucatan Peninsula). It

was by the geography of Ptolemy and Christopher Columbus that the pinpointing of Saint Thomas evangelizing the east was made.[16]

The Idea That Quetzalcoatl Was an Essene

There is certainly enough evidence to suggest that a pale, bearded prophet did exist, whoever he may have been. Perhaps he was even an Essene. The idea that Quetzalcoatl was an Essene was put forth by L. Taylor Hanson herself, the author of *He Walked the Americas*, for the Essenes always spoke of god as "My Father," just as Jesus did, and just as the Pale Prophet did.[17] They also favored a white, toga-like garment similar to the one the Pale Prophet is said to have worn. The Essenes were a Jewish sect who studied all the religions of the world, such as the teachings of the ancient Chaldeans, the teachings of Zoroaster, the secret instructions of Moses, and the revelations of Enoch. It is said they also studied the founding Masters of their order who had "transmitted techniques similar to those of Buddhism."[18] What began as a righteous movement of Judaism appears to have developed into a Buddhist-Jewish sect built on astrology, sun worship, and all their old Jewish traditions.

The Essenes believe they were called out from among the rest of society as God's favored people and thus moved out as missionaries to preach their philosophies to outlying colonies in various cities of Asia Minor. The Apostle Thomas is said to have taken some of the Essenes with him when he went to preach in South India in AD 52. A sect ultimately grew up there called the Saint Thomas Christians. While the Saint Thomas Christians did indeed favor Jesus, they considered segments of Hinduism equally viable in their search for God. The Hindus still hold the priests of the Saint Thomas Christians in high esteem and consider them to be holy men.[19]

One thing that is in favor of Quetzalcoatl being an Essene, or one of the members of the Saint Thomas Christian Church, is the route the Pale Prophet took on his travels. They appear to begin in the Polynesian islands, which could easily be reached from southern India. From there it is said that he followed the trade winds east across the Pacific Ocean to Peru. He then traveled to Brazil, the Caribbean, and into Central America and Mexico, and finally into the America southwest. Then he traveled to the Hopi, and among the Natives in the Northeast and in

Canada, before going back to Mexico. He stayed in Mexico until his ultimate departure when he headed east.[20]

The Symbol of the Cross

Another symbol of Saint Thomas that would help identify him as the Pale Prophet of legend was the cross—a symbol used by various bodies of Freemasonry, one of which is the Tau version of the cross with the top form missing.[21] The same Tau cross was engraven on the hand of the Pale Prophet. Crosses even encircled the hem of his white robe. The ornate cross, known as the Saint Thomas Cross, is found in a number of places in India, and is widely perceived as the symbol of the Saint Thomas Christians.[22] As the Pale Prophet moved through various crowds of worshipers, he always held up his hand with the strange palm markings that had the Tau cross engraved on it. He had taken it as his symbol. Yet never do we hear of the Pale Prophet asking anyone to feel the nail prints on his hands or feet, or to present a scar where a spear pierced his side (see John 19:34) in his efforts to prove his identity like Jesus did among the Nephites.

The Pale Prophet Identifies Himself as a Missionary

The strange palm markings of a cross on the palm of the Pale Prophet's hand only added to the speculation that he was the Savior, even though the native tribes understood it to represent the four directions.[23] Yet the Pale Prophet himself never suggested that he was anything other than a missionary. While visiting Peru, the Pale Prophet began to tell a strange story of a land across the sea where all the men were bearded like himself. He spoke of the people and customs and then spoke of a man who lived there that healed the people, taught them many things, and, in turn, was beloved by the people. He then proceeded to tell the entire story of his beloved Master Jesus Christ, including His death and Resurrection, saying in conclusion,

> Thus . . . does the Almighty protect the Man who carries his message, and not even one of earth's greatest nations in all its might has the power to kill Him while He follows the wishes of the Almighty.

> So too, is it with Me. And when just now the earth started shaking, it was to remind Me of this story which My Father had laid upon my heart to tell you so that you may know more about this Peace Religion.[24]

The fact that he was a mere mortal, not the immortal Jesus Christ, is noted in another episode in Peru, where the Pale Prophet is described as kneeling in prayer after being confronted by an army of angry men who questioned his ability to save himself. They said to him, "*You pretend to have power—then display it! Save yourself if you are able*!" Calling upon the Father in prayer, the prophet said, "*Oh, My Father, who art in Heaven, if it be thy will now to take me, and this be the manner—I am ready.*"[25] How can it be doubted that although a most holy follower of Christ, this saintly man, was not the Savior who had already been crucified and resurrected?

Mode of Travel and Other Inconsistencies

While the Savior appeared to the Nephites from out of heaven and slowly descended upon them, Kate-Zahl (the name by which the Pale Prophet was known in Mexico), traveled from place to place and from land to land by caravan or ship. Once he arrived, Kate-Zahl spent some time learning the language of the various tribes he visited so that he could teach them in their own language. This is not something the Savior would have had to do. While it can hardly be doubted that some of the legitimate tales of the Lord and His New World disciples got mixed up with tales of a pale prophet, there are too many inconsistencies to think the Lord or His twelve New World disciples were those detailed in some of the more prominent legends of Quetzalcoatl. None of them would have taught some of the things Quetzalcoatl is reportedly said to have taught—such as infant baptism, which is believed to have replaced infant sacrifice.

Infant Baptism

When asking about infant baptism, a Yaqui chieftain reportedly said to L. Taylor Hansen, "The baptismal? Yes. It was the Prophet who taught this. The godfather and godmother with their names of kinship; all must last for the life of the infant."[26] While baptism was an integral part of the worship of the Nephites, the Lord never would have taught that little children had to be baptized to gain entrance into heaven.

Listen to what the Lord taught His servants. In speaking to his son Moroni on the subject of baptism of little children, Mormon said,

> 8 Listen to the words of Christ, your Redeemer, your Lord and your God. Behold, I came into the world not to call the righteous but sinners to repentance; the whole need no physician, but they that are sick; wherefore, little children are whole, for they are not capable of committing sin; wherefore the curse of Adam is taken from them in me, that it hath no power over them; and the law of circumcision is done away in me.
>
> 9 And after this manner did the Holy Ghost manifest the word of God unto me; wherefore, my beloved son, I know that it is solemn mockery before God, that ye should baptize little children. (Moroni 8:5–9)

His Departure

The departure of the Pale Prophet was like that of any other man—not the Savior—for a great ship with a serpent's head guiding it forward ultimately arrived to carry him back home. People came from all directions to see the Pale Prophet off, knowing that this would be the last time they would see him. Songs and chants followed the procession that led him to the ship where the prophet, clad in his white robes that were encircled with black crosses,[27] raised his hands in a gesture of benediction and farewell to the crowds below. Before departing, he described a future world of peace where people would travel differently and dress differently. It would be a time of great peace and prosperity. In conclusion, he said, "Carry this vision on through the ages, and remember Kate-Zahl, the Prophet."[28]

L. Taylor Hansen, author of *He Walked the Americas,* said that Dr. Buck, curator of the Bishop Museum of Hawaii, noted that China had similar legends as did India. As to the identity of the Pale Prophet, Dr. Buck was unwilling to even guess.[29] His identity remains a mystery.

Notes

1. Torquemada quoted in Hubert Howe Bancroft, *The Works of Hubert Howe Bancroft: The Native Races* (San Francisco: A. L. Bancroft and Company, 1883), 3:255.
2. Mariano Veytia, *Ancient America Rediscovered,* compiled by Donald W. Hemingway and W. David Hemingway (Springville UT: Bonneville Books, 2000), 152.
3. Ibid.
4. John D. Baldwin, *Ancient America in Notes on American Archaeology* (CreateSpace, 2015), 201.
5. Hubert Howe Bancroft, *The Works of Hubert Howe Bancroft: The Native Races* (San Francisco: A. L. Bancroft and Company, 1883), 3:258.
6. Ibid., 3:192.
7. Ibid., 3:255.
8. Ibid., 3:260.
9. Ibid., 2:204.
10. L. Taylor Hansen, *He Walked the Americas* (Amherst WI: Legend Press, 1994), 67.
11. Roscoe Pound, *Lectures on Masonic Jurisprudence,* Little Masonic Library, no. 4 (Macoy Publishing, 1977,) 4:32 in "Masons (Freemasonry): Christian or Anti-Christian?," *rapidnet.com*, accessed March 16, 2017, rapidnet.com/~jbeard/bdm/Cults/masons.htm.
12. Christine Berta, "Biography: St. Thomas the Apostle," *St. Thomas the Apostle Catholic Church*, accessed March 16, 2017, www.stapostle.org/st-thomas-church-parish-history/saint-thomas-biography/.
13. Abbot George Burke, "The Apostle of India," *Original Christianity and Original Yoga*, accessed March 16, 2017, ocoy.org/original-christianity/apostle-of-india/.
14. Robert Eric Frykenberg, *Christianity in India: From Beginnings to the Present* (Oxford: Oxford University Press, 2008), 100.

15. Hubert Howe Bancroft, *The Works of Hubert Howe Bancroft: The Native Races* (San Francisco: A. L. Bancroft and Company, 1883), 3:456.

16. "Quetzalcoatl: Man or Myth?," *123helpme!.com*, accessed March 16, 2017, 123helpme.com/view.asp?id=82876.

17. L. Taylor Hansen, *He Walked the Americas* (Amherst WI: Legend Press, 1994).

18. "Who Were the Essenes?," *Essene Spirit*, accessed March 16, 2017, essenespirit.com/who.html.

19. *Wikipedia*, s.v. "Saint Thomas Christians," last modified March 1, 2017, en.wikipedia.org/wiki/Saint_Thomas_Christians.

20. L. Taylor Hansen, *He Walked the Americas* (Amherst WI: Legend Press, 1994), 196.

21. *Masonic Dictionary Online*, s.v. "Tau," accessed March 24, 2017, www.masonicdictionary.com/tau.html. See also *Masonic Dictionary Online*, s.v. "Crosses," accessed March 24, 2017, www.masonicdictionary.com/crosses.html.

22. "Masons (Freemasonry): Christian or Anti-Christian?," *rapidnet.com*, accessed March 16, 2017, rapidnet.com/~jbeard/bdm/Cults/masons.htm.

23. L. Taylor Hansen, *He Walked the Americas* (Amherst WI: Legend Press, 1994), 34.

24. Ibid., 153.

25. Ibid., 157.

26. Ibid., 112.

27. Ibid., 191.

28. Ibid., 172.

29. L. Taylor Hansen, *He Walked the Americas* (Amherst WI: Legend Press, 1994), 205.

8

The Rise of the Gentiles

In the sad hours and years that followed the horrific battle at Cumorah, Moroni recorded not only the epilogue to his own people's destruction, but the fate that befell the Jaredites as well. In so doing, he was quick to remind us that their destruction came about because they had forsaken the Lord and had all turned to sin. "For behold, they rejected all the words of Ether; for he truly told them of all things, from the beginning of man; and that after the waters had receded from off the face of this land it became a choice land above all other lands, a chosen land of the Lord; wherefore the Lord would have that all men should serve him who dwell upon the face thereof" (Ether 13:2).

The Nephites were next to inherit the land, and they, too, were warned of the terrible consequence if they turned from God: "Wherefore, this land is consecrated unto him whom he shall bring. And if it so be that they shall serve him according to the commandments which he hath given, it shall be a land of liberty unto them; wherefore, they shall never be brought down into captivity; if so, it shall be because of iniquity; for if iniquity shall abound cursed shall be the land for their sakes, but unto the righteous it shall be blessed forever" (2 Nephi 1:7).

Many promises were made to both nations, but in each instance, the children of the promised land ultimately turned their backs on God and served the devil instead. The Lord reminded them over and over again that they must keep the promised land clean, so that at some future time the great Gentile nation, which was destined to rise in the latter days, would be able to fulfill its mission—preparing the way for the

Restoration of all things in anticipation of the Savior's Second Advent. Unfortunately, neither nation remained faithful, and both were totally wiped away—including almost all evidence of their very existence, lest others desire the land for its riches before the appointed time of the Gentiles. The Jaredites were destroyed down to two men, Coriantmur and the prophet Ether. Only Moroni survived among the Nephites slaughtered at Cumorah, and, of course, the victorious Lamanites who, in deference to certain prophets who pled their case, would be permitted continued existence in the land. Unfortunately, because the Nephites had been given greater light and knowledge than the Lamanites, and had then turned away from it, they were not privileged to such consideration.

Seven Fires Prophecy of the Anishinaabe

The Lord so loved the seed of Lehi that He promised that America would remain the land of their inheritance forever. Unfortunately, with the time quickly approaching for the Gentiles to take possession of the land as its next inheritors, the Lord could see that the Lamanites were in jeopardy of, not just losing a large number of their people, but of total annihilation. Thus, He sent prophets to warn them of the impending danger, just as He did centuries earlier among their ancestral fathers. The Anishinaabe living along the Atlantic coast speak of eight spiritual beings, or prophets, who appeared to them over seven periods of time. Each period was called a Fire, and each prophet in each period warned the Anishinaabe of future events.

Oral traditions say the only tribe to hear the first prophet was the Micmac. Interestingly, the Micmac were among the first tribes encountered by Europeans. When John Cabot made his first English voyage to North America (in 1497), which resulted in the discovery of the Labrador coast of Newfoundland.[1] He took three natives back to England with them, who are now believed to have been Micmac.[2] The seven remaining prophets were sent to the rest of the Anishinaabe tribes at various time thereafter. The Anishinaabe were in danger of being slaughtered as more and more colonies of incoming Europeans began to descend upon the area and often saw the Native Americans as nothing more than savages.

THE FIRST FIRE PROPHECY

In the time of the *First Fire* (around AD 1400), the Anishinaabe, who had been living peacefully along the Atlantic coast for centuries, were encouraged to move farther inland, for the prophet warned that their way of life would soon come to an end. They were told they would be guided to seven stopping places along their way, each marked by a sacred Megis shell. Their final stopping point would be a place where food grows on water (Lake Superior, where wild rice grows on water). They were advised, in the interest of security, to divide into two groups. One would leave and go deep into the interior of the continent and wait until the intentions of the light-skinned race were made known. The other group would wait and greet the newcomers as brother and sister. Thus, after asking permission of their allied Abenaki brothers to travel through their territory, ten thousand canoes of the first division could be seen traveling west along the St. Lawrence River to the Ottawa River, then to Lake Nipissing, and on to the Great Lakes.[3]

THE SECOND AND THIRD FIRE PROPHECIES

The Second and Third Fire prophecies provided additional instructions and council for the westward migration. Several stopping places along the way included the Ottawa River and around Niagara Falls, and westward near the Detroit River in southern Ontario. This part of the migration alone took many generations to complete because they settled in each of the places they stopped. Thus, by the time the Anishinaabe reached the Detroit River, they had already divided into six separate nations: the Algonquian, Nipissing, Mississauga, Ojibway, Odawa, and Potawatomi.[4] The Ojibway, the third largest group of Native Americans north of Mexico, ultimately settled near Sault Ste. Marie in Ontario: a settlement that is southward to the Ohio River, along the Illinois River and westward along the northern Great Lakes. The Ojibway were keepers of the books and kept detailed and complex scrolls of events, history, songs, maps, memories, stories, geometries, and mathematics. Thus, we can suppose that the Ojibway were chiefly of Nephite stock, for the scriptures tell us that of the many Nephites who moved north and mingled with the Lamanites, it was chiefly the Nephites who kept the records (see Helaman 3:15). Their records proved their devotion to God, or the Great Spirit. William Warren, who spent many years among the Ojibway, said,

> It is a general fact that most people who have been discovered living in a savage and unenlightened state, and even whole nations living in

> partial civilization have been found to be idolaters—having no just conception of a great first Cause or Creator, invisible to human eyes and pervading all space. With the Ojibways it is not so; the fact of their firm belief and great veneration, in an overruling Creator and Master of Life, has been noticed by all who have had close intercourse with them since their earliest discovery. It is true that they believe in a multiplicity of spirits which pervade all nature, yet all these are subordinate to the one Great Spirit of good.[5]

THE FOURTH FIRE PROPHECY

During the *Fourth Fire*, information was given to them about the arrival of white people who would come bringing new knowledge and promises of great blessings, a people who were destined to grow into a mighty nation.[6] (With the rise of the Gentile nation, this prophecy has now been fulfilled.)

THE FIFTH FIRE PROPHECY

The Anishinaabe were told that in the *Fifth Fire* great struggles would come upon all the native people because many would accept the promises of the white man and would abandon their old ways of life. Moreover, all those who accepted the promise would cause the near extinction of their people, with great struggles following that would remain with them for many generations.[7] (Once the descendants of the Anishinaabe melded into the mainstream of America, their identity and culture has been all but lost—just as prophesied.)

THE SIXTH FIRE PROPHECY

The sixth prophet told the Anishinaabe that in the time of the *Sixth Fire* it would become evident that they had been deceived by the earlier promises and that a bitter time would follow. They were foretold that their grandsons and granddaughters would turn upon their Elders who would then lose their reason for living.[8] Thus, the time of the sixth fire would be a time of great struggles for their people, with the cup of life becoming the cup of grief.

THE SEVENTH FIRE PROPHECY

The seventh prophet was somewhat different from the early prophets. This prophet was "young and had a strange light in his eyes." He spoke of a new people who would emerge. These new people would be instrumental in bringing their people back to life. His prophetic warnings were also somewhat different than those of the other six prophets, for they were not just meant for the Anishinaabe, but for all those living in America today. He warned those in the present to either put away their wicked ways and come together for the mutual benefit and healing of all people and also of Mother Earth, or great destructions and woes would follow.[9]

The Rise of the Gentiles

With the fall of the Nephite nation, and with those on the east coast being directed to safer territory, the Lord began the process of preparing the way for the influx of Gentiles who were next in line to inherit the promised land. But, just like the Nephites and Jaredites before them, the blessings the Gentiles would enjoy would be conditional upon their righteousness and their worship of the Lord, Jesus Christ. This great land of liberty cannot stand without the blessings of the Almighty. Ezra Taft Benson said,

> Many great events have transpired in this land of destiny. This was the place where Adam dwelt; this was the place where the Garden of Eden was; it was here that Adam met with a body of high priests at Adam-ondi-Ahman shortly before his death and gave them his final blessing, and the place to which he will return to meet with the leaders of his people (D&C 107:53–57). This was the place of three former civilizations: that of Adam, that of the Jaredites, and that of the Nephites. This was also the place where our Heavenly Father and his Son, Jesus Christ, appeared to Joseph Smith, inaugurating the last dispensation.
>
> The Lord has also decreed that this land should be "the place of the new Jerusalem, which should come down out of heaven, and the holy sanctuary of the Lord" (Ether 13:3). Here is our nation's destiny! To serve God's eternal purposes and to prepare this land and people for America's eventual destiny, He "established the Constitution of this land, by the hands of wise men whom [He] raised up unto this very purpose, and redeemed the land by the shedding of blood." (D&C 101:80)[10]

In 2 Nephi 10 we learn several things that identify the promised land as America, with the Gentiles the next in line to enjoy its blessings:

> 10 But behold, this land, said God, shall be a land of thine inheritance, and the Gentiles shall be blessed upon the land.
>
> 11 And this land shall be a land of liberty unto the Gentiles, and there shall be no kings upon the land, who shall raise up unto the Gentiles.
>
> 12 And I will fortify this land against all other nations.
>
> 13 And he that fighteth against Zion shall perish, saith God.
>
> 14 For he that raiseth up a king against me shall perish, for I, the Lord, the king of heaven, will be their king, and I will be a light unto them forever, that hear my words. (2 Nephi 10:10–14)

Far too many scriptures describe the greatness of the latter-day Gentile nation to have any questions about the location of the promised land. Right from the beginning, America was destined to rise with an influx of pilgrims from many nations under the care of founding fathers who would formulate a Constitution of the people, by the people, and for the people (see 1 Nephi 2:20; 2 Nephi 1: 3–5, 7–8; Ether 13:2–3, 6, 8–12). Joseph Fielding Smith tells us that the Lord raised up such honorable men to assure that America remain a land of freedom. Joseph Fielding Smith said,

> The founders of this nation were men of humble faith. Many of them saw in vision a glorious destiny for our government, provided we would faithfully continue in the path of justice and right with contrite spirits and humble hearts, accepting the divine truths which are found in the holy scriptures. The appeal of these men has echoed down the passing years with prophetic warning to the succeeding generations, pleading with them to be true to all these standards which lay at the foundation of our government.
>
> This country was founded as a Christian nation, with the acceptance of Jesus Christ as the Redeemer of the world. It was predicted by a prophet of old that this land would be a land of liberty and would be fortified against all other nations as long as its inhabitants would serve Jesus Christ; but would they stray from the Son of God, it would cease to be a land of liberty and his anger be kindled against them.[11]

Ezra Taft Benson also taught, "Our nation, the United States of America, was built on the foundation of reality and spirituality. To the extent that its citizens violate God's commandments, especially His laws of morality—to that degree they weaken the country's foundation. A rejection and repudiation of God's laws could well lead our nation to its destruction just as it has to Greece and Rome. It can happen to our country unless we repent."[12]

Blessings and Cursings

The blessings and cursings pronounced upon those who occupy the land of promise were rehearsed to the Nephites during their earliest years in the land. The Nephites were told early so that throughout the generations they would know that the promised land was *holy ground* and must not be defiled. We learn of its status as holy ground from Enos, "And while I was thus struggling in the spirit, behold, the voice of the Lord came into my mind again, saying: I will visit thy brethren according to their diligence in keeping my commandments. I have given unto them this land, and it is a holy land; and I curse it not save it be for the cause of iniquity; wherefore, I will visit thy brethren according as I have said; and their transgressions will I bring down with sorrow upon their own heads" (Enos 1:10).

The prophecies pertinent to this holy land of America were not just directed to the ancient Saints, but to those of our day as well, so we too might know of our responsibility to keep the promised land free from sin. Great blessings have been bestowed upon the Gentiles of this generation. Yet, the scriptures make it clear that the land will be cursed if those who have been led to this land turn to iniquity.

> 5 But, said he, notwithstanding our afflictions, we have obtained a land of promise, a land which is choice above all other lands; a land which the Lord God hath covenanted with me should be a land for the inheritance of my seed. Yea, the Lord hath covenanted this land unto me, and to my children forever, and also all those who should be led out of other countries by the hand of the Lord.
>
> 6 Wherefore, I, Lehi, prophesy according to the workings of the Spirit which is in me, that there shall none come into this land save they shall be brought by the hand of the Lord.
>
> 7 Wherefore, this land is consecrated unto him whom he shall bring. And if it so be that they shall serve him according to the commandments which he hath given, it shall be a land of liberty unto them; wherefore, they shall never be brought down into captivity; if so, it shall be because of iniquity; for if iniquity shall abound cursed shall be the land for their sakes, but unto the righteous it shall be blessed forever. (2 Nephi 1:5–7)

The Founding of America

Speaking across the pulpit in the October 1987 general conference, Prophet Ezra Taft Benson said,

> Two great American Christian civilizations—the Jaredites and the Nephites—were swept off this land because they did not "serve the God of the land, who is Jesus Christ" (Ether 2:12). What will become of our civilization? . . .
>
> For centuries the Lord kept America hidden in the hollow of His hand until the time was right to unveil her for her destiny in the last days. "It is wisdom that this land should be kept as yet from the knowledge of other nations," said Lehi, "for behold, many nations would overrun the land, that there would be no place for an inheritance" (2 Nephi 1:8).
>
> In the Lord's due time His Spirit "wrought upon" . . . the pilgrims, the Puritans, and others to come to America. They testified of God's intervention in their behalf (see 1 Nephi 13:12–13). The Book of Mormon records that they humbled "themselves before the Lord; and the power of the Lord was with them" (1 Nephi 13:16).
>
> Our Father in Heaven planned the coming forth of the Founding Fathers and their form of government as the necessary great prologue leading to the restoration of the gospel. Recall what our Savior Jesus Christ said nearly two thousand years ago when He visited this promised land: "For it is wisdom in the Father that they should be established in this land, and be set up as a free people by the power of the Father, that these things might come forth" (3 Nephi 21:4). America, the land of liberty, was to be the Lord's latter-day base of operations for His restored church.[13]

The Iroquois League of Nations

Interestingly, the Iroquois (a descending branch of the seed of Lehi) had much to do with the formation of our form of government. The Iroquois have been described as a barbarous people, yet they exhibited a noble genius. According to early American colonists, they were polite and managed all their affairs judiciously. With the Restoration of the gospel only a few centuries away, work had to be done to prepare the promised land for the rise of the new Gentile nation—a nation that had to be founded upon the principles of equality and justice so that the Restoration could take place. Thus, the Lord raised up Hiawatha—a great Onondaga orator who was instrumental in setting the stage for this nation's rise to power as a land of liberty among the Gentiles. It all began with the formation of a unique League of Nations, which Hiawatha first presented to his own people in New York (near the region of the Finger Lakes, not too far from the Hill Cumorah). The Iroquois League of Nations came about at a time when many of the Iroquois tribes of New York were warring among their own five nations. To make matters worse, they were surrounded by the Algonquian on all sides. The Algonquian made unwanted incursions into the Iroquois territory and caused even more friction and bloodshed.

Three main figures show up in the story of the formation of the Iroquois' League of Nations.

ATOTARHO

The first man in the story of this formation practiced the dark arts and took out whole families by way of secret murders, which suggests ties to the Gadiantons. The central nation, the Onondagas, were then under the control of a dreaded chief, whose name is variously given, Atotarho, Watatotahlo, or Tododaho, according to the dialect of the speaker and the orthography of the writer. Atotarho, as we shall call him, was described as a wizard: a fierce man so hated that he was depicted in their artwork as having hair comprised of swarms of writhing snakes (a not so pretty picture, but one that was fitting). He was described as haughty, stern, crafty, and as a remorseless tyrant. It is said that he could kill people even at a distance by virtue of his magic arts. Not surprisingly, no one wanted to cross him because he didn't tolerate equality and he killed anyone who attempted to rise above him. Satan was once again doing his best to thwart the work of God by using those steeped in magic and witchcraft to do his bidding.[14]

HIAWATHA

The second leading figure in the founding of the Iroquois League was Hiawatha, an Onondaga chief of high rank, past middle age, but greatly loved by his people because of his benevolent nature and wisdom. Unfortunately, a time came when he was consumed by grief because many of his friends and family members (including all his daughters) had been killed by the wicked sorcerer Atotarho, although he himself had been spared. He also felt the pains of his people who were suffering untold misery because of the never-ending wars that were tearing his nation apart. Thus, he spent a considerable amount of time in contemplation, devising an elaborate scheme for a vast confederacy that would ensure his people lasting peace. Most of the tribes had already been involved in one type of confederacy or another, but the one he envisioned would not be a loose transitory league, but a permanent government. He hoped that it would involve all the tribes and abolish war altogether.

After working out the particulars in his own mind, Hiawatha presented the plan to his people in a grand council meeting. Unfortunately, Atotarho sat at the back, and his fearsome appearance and scowl of disapproval totally overwhelmed the congregation, causing them to back away from the proposal. A second counsel was called, and once more Hiawatha attempted to get his tribesmen's approval. But once again, Atotarho's scornful face was seen in the crowd, and once again, the people backed away. When a third attempt failed to bring even one person to the meeting, Hiawatha left disheartened. He sat down on the ground and buried his head in the folds of his mantle. He remained there for a long time, bowed down in grief and sorrow. After composing himself, he arose and headed out of town toward the southeast.[15]

THE GREAT PEACEMAKER, DEGANAWIDA

At length, Hiawatha came to a Mohawk town where he hoped to converse with chief Deganawida, an Onondaga by birth, but who had been adopted by the Mohawk.[16] Deganawida's fame ranks right along with Hiawatha and Atotarho as the third person of interest in this story. Deganawida was born into the Huron branch of the Iroquois living just to the north of Lake Ontario in what is today Kingston, Ontario. He arrived in New York after crossing Lake Ontario in a white canoe. He is described as a most holy man who was known for his powerful visions. Deganawida's role was not that of a warrior but of a redemptive shaman. Even as a child, Deganawida spoke of finding a peaceful way for the tribes to coexist because they were constantly at war with one another. If only they could coexist in peace. Hiawatha felt that if he could entice Deganawida to at least hear about the confederacy, Deganawida might help the league come to fruition. Thus Hiawatha seated himself on a log and waited for those from Deganawida's village to pass by on their way to draw water.

In time, one of the tribesmen came out with his vessel for water and approached the spring where Hiawatha was seated. Hiawatha said nothing and sat motionless. Yet there was something in his demeanor that elicited great awe in the tribesman, and he went back to the village to tell of the event, noting every detail of the stranger, even down to the string of white shells Hiawatha had made along the way and placed around his neck. Deganawida suggested that he must be a guest, and bid the tribesman go fetch Hiawatha and bring him back to the village. And thus the two chiefs met and found in each other kindred spirits. Deganawida took to Hiawatha's plan immediately, and after perfecting it between themselves they presented it to the other tribes. It was ultimately accepted because the plan enunciated principles of justice and equality and made it clear that the bloodshed among the tribes must yield to a new sense of brotherhood.[17]

THE LAW OF PEACE

This new Law of Peace laid out a government of the people, by the people, and for the people, with three branches—each of which amounted to a faith based on reason and thinking. Deganawida then described a great *Tree of Peace* under whose branches the tribes would meet to resolve their differences. Together, he and Hiawatha converted each of the tribes to this new Law of Peace. This law became the foundation of the Iroquois League of Nations.

FORGING ALLIANCES

Deganawida and Hiawatha traveled the length and breadth of Iroquois country, forging alliances, and teaching the laws of justice. One by one, each village and town was converted to this new change in government and eventually met at Onondaga Lake in New York for a grand council of the newly united nations. The first meeting was held by fifty chiefs under a giant evergreen tree. Deganawida is said to have uprooted a white pine tree, exposing a deep cavern with a river at its bottom. He instructed his warriors to cast their weapons into this hole and then watch as the river carried them deep into the bowels of the earth. Replanting the tree, the prophet said, "This burying the hatchet is the end of killing and war."[18]

The practice of burying their weapons of war was first introduced to their ancestral fathers back in the Book of Mormon when the Lamanites (who were converted to the doctrines of Christ) buried their weapons and refused to take them up again, even in the face of death (see Alma 24:16–17).

How can anyone miss the similarities between this burying the hatchet and the episode in the Book of Mormon where the converted Lamanites buried their weapons of war—a tradition which appears to have been carried through the generations to Deganawida's day?

> 14 And the great God has had mercy on us, and made these things known unto us that we might not perish; yea, and he has made these things known unto us beforehand, because he loveth our souls as well as he loveth our children; therefore, in his mercy he doth visit us by his angels, that the plan of salvation might be made known unto us as well as unto future generations. . . .
>
> 16 And now, my brethren, if our brethren seek to destroy us, behold, we will hide away our swords, yea, even we will bury them deep in the earth, that they may be kept bright, as a testimony that we have never used them, at the last day; and if our brethren destroy us, behold, we shall go to our God and shall be saved.
>
> 17 And now it came to pass that when the king had made an end of these sayings, and all the people were assembled together, they took their swords, and all the weapons which were used for the shedding of man's blood, and they did bury them up deep in the earth.
>
> 19 And thus we see that, when these Lamanites were brought to believe and to know the truth, they were firm, and would suffer even unto death rather than commit sin; and thus we see that they buried their weapons of peace, or they buried the weapons of war, for peace. (Alma 24:14, 16–17, 19)

The Founding Fathers of America

Hiawatha's vision of a united confederacy, which was put into practice by Deganawida, ultimately put an end to much of the incessant feuding between the tribes. But the combined strength of the league gave the Iroquois a dominance that continued to shape the region's history for years to come. In fact, the Founding Fathers of America found that their best working model for their new government was not in the writings of European nations, but within the Iroquois League. The Great Law of Peace provided both model and incentive to transform thirteen separate colonies into the United States.

The Tree of Peace ultimately became the Tree of Liberty, and the eagle (clutching a bundle of thirteen arrows) became the symbol of the new American government. Thus, the Iroquois were instrumental in the formation of our own government.

David Yarrow said,

> The Iroquois Confederacy existed centuries before the U.S. Constitution was written. Historians, anthropologists, and traditional chiefs addressed the proposal the U.S. Constitution was based on the Iroquois Great Law of Peace rather than on Greek democracy, as is commonly believed and taught. . . .
>
> The modern age of democracy had its origin in the vast recesses of this continent, and from here it spread throughout the world. American democracy owes its distinctive character of debate and compromise to the principles and structure of American Indian civil government.[19]

Our Country's Founders Also Warned the Nation

Our Founding Fathers were very much aware of the Lord's part in the formation of this country and of the necessity of keeping God in the forefront of our lives. The words of Dr. Daniel Webster, who spoke to the New York Historical Society on February 22, 1852 (Washington's birthday), is as pertinent to those of our day as it was to those of his. He said,

> Unborn ages and visions of glory crowd upon my soul, the realization of all which, however, is in the hands and good pleasure of Almighty God; but, under his divine blessing, it will be dependent on the character and the virtues of ourselves, and of our posterity. . . . And let me say, gentlemen, that if we and our posterity shall be true to the Christian religion—if we and they shall live always in the fear of God, and shall respect his commandments, if we and they shall maintain just, moral sentiments, and such conscientious convictions of duty as shall control the heart and life—we may have the highest hopes of the future fortunes of our country; and if we maintain those institutions of government and that political union, exceeding all praise as much as it exceeds all former examples of political associations, we may be sure of one thing—that while our country furnishing materials for a thousand masters of the historic art, it will afford no topic for a Gibbon. It will have no Decline and Fall. It will go on prospering and to prosper.

> But, if we and our posterity reject religious instruction and authority, violate the rules of eternal justice, trifle with the injunctions of morality, and recklessly destroy the political constitution which holds us together, no man can tell how sudden a catastrophe may overwhelm us, that shall bury all our glory in profound obscurity. Should that catastrophe happen, let it have no history! Let the horrible narrative never be written! Let its fate be like that of the lost books of Livy, which no human eye shall ever read; or the missing Pleiad, of which no man can ever know more, than that it is lost, and lost forever![20]

His foreboding warning may well come to fruition if we continue down the same path. The fate of the country would be so terrible if we fail in our duties to both God and man. Even reading about it would be too painful to endure.

General Douglas MacArthur spoke of his own concerns about the need to keep our country's moral integrity intact, including our dependence on God. He said in *A Soldier Speaks*, on December 12, 1951,

> In this day of gathering storms, as the moral deterioration of political power spreads its growing infection, it is essential that every spiritual force be mobilized to defend and preserve the religious base upon which this nation was founded. For it is that base which has been the motivating impulse to our moral and national growth. History fails to record a single precedent in which nations subject to moral decay have not passed into political and economic decline. There has been either a spiritual reawakening to overcome the moral lapse, or a progressive deterioration leading to ultimate national disaster. . . . The hour is late, the time is short. We must begin now, in earnest, and invite God's blessings on our efforts.[21]

The Lessons of the Past

Having both been totally destroyed, it is sad to note that the Nephites and the Jaredites learned the hard way just how serious the Lord was about keeping the promised land clean and firmly rooted in its Christian foundation. Both fatally learned that as people grow they follow one of two paths: either upward to God, or down to destruction. Ezra Taft Benson noted that history itself proves nations' progress

> From bondage to spiritual faith
> From spiritual faith to courage
> From courage to freedom

From freedom to abundance
From abundance to selfishness
From selfishness to complacency
From complacency to apathy
From apathy to fear
From fear to dependency
From dependency to bondage.[22]

The same thing was taught back in the Book of Mormon where we read,

> 2 Yea, and we may see at the very time when he doth prosper his people, yea, in the increase of their fields, their flocks and their herds, and in gold, and in silver, and in all manner of precious things of every kind and art; sparing their lives, and delivering them out of the hands of their enemies; softening the hearts of their enemies that they should not declare wars against them; yea, and in fine, doing all things for the welfare and happiness of his people; yea, then is the time that they do harden their hearts, and do forget the Lord their God, and do trample under their feet the Holy One—yea, and this because of their ease, and their exceedingly great prosperity.
>
> 3 And thus we see that except the Lord doth chasten his people with many afflictions, yea, except he doth visit them with death and with terror, and with famine and with all manner of pestilence, they will not remember him.
>
> 4 O how foolish, and how vain, and how evil, and devilish, and how quick to do iniquity, and how slow to do good, are the children of men; yea, how quick to hearken unto the words of the evil one, and to set their hearts upon the vain things of the world! (Helaman 12:2–4)

Searching the Book of Mormon for the enlightenment we need to survive the coming storms is not just a request from the Lord himself, but also from our living prophets. It is a plea from Mormon and Moroni and all those who fought and died in battle to preserve these records so that those of our day might learn from the mistakes of the past and not fall victim to Satin's wiles. The lament of Mormon as he witnessed the destruction of his people from the top of the Hill Cumorah is heart-wrenching and should be a warning to those of our day who could face a similar fate if they do not repent and return to God. Mormon said,

> 17 O ye fair ones, how could ye have departed from the ways of the Lord! O ye fair ones, how could ye have rejected that Jesus, who stood with open arms to receive you!
>
> 18 Behold, if ye had not done this, ye would not have fallen. But behold, ye are fallen, and I mourn your loss.
>
> 19 O ye fair sons and daughters, ye fathers and mothers, ye husbands and wives, ye fair ones, how is it that ye could have fallen!
>
> 20 But behold, ye are gone, and my sorrows cannot bring your return.
>
> 21 And the day soon cometh that your mortal must put on immortality, and these bodies which are now moldering in corruption must soon become incorruptible bodies; and then ye must stand before the judgment-seat of Christ, to be judged according to your works; and if it so be that ye are righteous, then are ye blessed with your fathers who have gone before you.
>
> 22 O that ye had repented before this great destruction had come upon you. But behold, ye are gone, and the Father, yea, the Eternal Father of heaven, knoweth your state; and he doeth with you according to his justice and mercy. (Mormon 6:17–22)

Hopefully, with the scriptures to guide us and remind us of the past, this generation can avoid the pitfalls that caused so much sorrow and destruction in the past, and can look forward with joyful anticipation for the Savior's prophesied Second Coming.

Notes

1. "John Cabot," *Royal Museums Greenwich*, accessed March 24, 2017, www.rmg.co.uk/discover/explore/john-cabot.
2. Daniel S. Murphree, ed., *Native America: A State-by-State Historical Encyclopedia*, vol. 1, *Alabama–Louisiana* (Santa Barbara, CA: Greenwood, 2012), 472.
3. *Wikipedia*, s.v. "Seven fires prophecy," last modified February 21, 2017, en.wikipedia.org/wiki/Seven_fires_prophecy. Tom Dostou, "Seven Fires Prophecy of the Anishnabe People and the Process of Reconciliation," *Prayer Vigil for the Earth*, July 11, 2000, accessed March 24, 2017, oneprayer.org/SevenFiresProphecyAnishnabePeople.html.
4. *Wikipedia*, s.v. "Seven fires prophecy," last modified February 21, 2017, en.wikipedia.org/wiki/Seven_fires_prophecy.
5. William W. Warren, *History of the Ojibway People*, 2nd ed. (St. Paul: Minnesota Historical Society, 2009), 55.
6. Ibid.
7. Ibid.
8. Ibid.
9. Ibid.
10. Ezra Taft Benson, *The Teachings of Ezra Taft Benson* (Salt Lake City: Bookcraft, 1988), 587–88.
11. Joseph Fielding Smith, *Doctrines of Salvation*, comp. Bruce R. McConkie (Salt Lake City: Bookcraft, 1956), 3:325.
12. Ezra Taft Benson, *The Teachings of Ezra Taft Benson* (Salt Lake City: Bookcraft, 1988), 571.
13. Ezra Taft Benson, "Our Divine Constitution," *Ensign*, November 1987.
14. "Hiawatha and the Iroquois Confederation," Horatio Hale, *Mark Shepard's Peace Page*, accessed March 24, 2017, www.markshep.com/peace/Hiawatha.html.
15. Ibid.

16. *Wikipedia*, s.v. "Great Peacemaker," last modified February 8, 2017, en.wikipedia.org/wiki/Great_Peacemaker.
17. "Hiawatha and the Iroquois Confederation," Horatio Hale, *Mark Shepard's Peace Page*, accessed March 24, 2017, www.markshep .com/peace/Hiawatha.html.
18. "Tree of Peace and Caduceus," *dyarrow.org*, accessed March 24, 2017, www.dyarrow.org/indigenous/caduseus.htm.
19. "The Great Law of Peace: New World Roots of American Democracy," David Yarrow, *dyarrow.org*, accessed March 23, 2017, www.dyarrow.org/indigenous/greatlaw.htm.
20. B. H. Roberts, *New Witnesses for God: The Book of Mormon* (Salt Lake City: Deseret News, 1951), 3:321–22.
21. Edward T. Imparto, comp., *General MacArthur: Wisdom and Visions* (Kentucky: Turner Publishing, 2000), 129.
22. Ezra Taft Benson, *An Enemy Hath Done This*, compiled by Jerreld L. Newquist (Salt Lake City: Parliament Publishers, 1969), 117.

9

Native American Prophecies

When European colonists first arrived in this promised land of America they described it as a beautiful, unspoiled wilderness—a virtual paradise. It was largely because the Native Americans had learned to live in harmony with the earth. These Native Americans tried to show the colonists some of their time-honored agricultural practices, such as adding the remains of a fish to fertilize and ensure the growth of their crops. The Native Americans tried to explain that you have to feed the earth if you want it to produce, but the colonists saw such customs as savage and beneath them. While the colonists' crops grew for a time, after several years the soil in many areas was so depleted of its nutrients that nothing grew anymore. The Chippewa teacher of Ojibway stock, Sun Bear, said, "These people just wore out the soil. They never bothered to take care of it or to use proper crop practices. As a result, they had to keep moving westward in order to have productive farmland. And as they went, they continued to cut down trees and kill Indians. Almost all of the beautiful forests that had been here for thousands of years were destroyed at that time. Massive deforestation and genocide were part of the famous, "glorious" movement westward."[1]

The Natives had no concept of owning the lands they lived, died, and were buried on. Every bit of the land was sacred to the Indians. They thought the Europeans would use the land in the same way that they did, but that was not the case. Soon the Indians were being displaced or killed in order to free up more land for the colonists. Read the following response to all of this by the Iroquois orator, Red Jacket, who is to be considered one of the best orators of his time.

Red Jacket's Lament

> Friend and Brother, it was the will of the Great Spirit that we meet together this day. . . .
>
> Brother this council fire was kindled by you. . . .
>
> Brother, listen to what we say. There was a time when our forefathers owned this great land. Their seats extended from the rising to the setting sun. The Great Spirit had made it for the use of the Indians. He had created the buffalo, the deer, and other animals for food. He had made the bear and the beaver, and their skins served us for clothing. He had scattered them over the country, and taught us how to take them. . . . If we had any disputes about hunting grounds, they were generally settled without the shedding of much blood; but an evil day came upon us; your forefathers crossed the great waters, and landed on this island. Their numbers were small; they found tribes, and not enemies; they told us they had fled from their own country for fear of wicked men, and come here to enjoy their religions. They asked for a small seat; we took pity on them, granted their request, and they sat down among us; we gave them corn and meat; they gave us poison in return.
>
> The white people had now found our country, tidings were carried back, and more came among us, yet we did not fear them, we took them to be our friends. . . . They wanted more land; they wanted our country. Our eyes were opened, and our minds became uneasy. Wars took place; Indians were hired to fight against Indians; and many of our people were destroyed. They also brought strong liquors among us; it was strong and powerful, and has slain thousands.
>
> Brother, our seats were once large, and yours were very small; you have now become a great people, and we have scarcely a place left to spread our blankets; you have got our country.[2]

In time, the natural resources (including gold, silver, and copper) brought a number of European nations to the shores of America. These newcomers are those referred to as the Gentile nation in the Book of Mormon. The attitude toward the Native American people was one of fear and contempt. Thus, over the course of the next two or three centuries, the Indian population dropped from some three million people to thirty thousand. In some cases, whole Indians tribes were completely wiped out.

Sun Bear said,

> I'm going to share with you a prophecy of my own people, the Ojibwa. This is a prophecy told to us by our great ancestors through our pictographs. They saw the coming of the Europeans to this continent. They saw the kind of hats they would be wearing. They saw how they would look and the kind of canoes they would have. They were told that if these people came in a sacred manner and accepted the knowledge that was given to them by the people of this continent, then it would be a beautiful thing. We would walk as brothers and sisters on the land.
>
> It soon became obvious that the Europeans didn't respect the sacred teachings of the land. Our prophecies said that if this happened, there would come a time when we would lie in the dust for 100 years or more as if we were dead. Even our own people wouldn't resect our teachings, and both Native and non-Native people would fail to understand them. Some Natives would turn from the teachings and be lured away saying, "This is a better teaching."
>
> Our prophecies also said that at the end of that 100 years, we would be walking on our hind legs again. We would be alive as if we were Earth spirits just reborn. We'd stand up and have our power again. . . .
>
> At that time, our sons and daughters would again come to us and ask to be taught the sacred ways. And the sons and daughters of the people who had come across the Great Water would come to us, too. They would say, "Teach us, for we are about to destroy the Earth." This is the stage we are at right now.[3]

Today, the Gentiles have full control of America, and the Indians believe America is now singing its death song. Changes in global weather conditions are on the minds of not just those in our nation, but in prominent nations around the world who fear that the natural disasters produced by such changes could have catastrophic affects for us all. Yet, Sun Bear also saw political chaos in our future. He said: "I see a lot of political unrest and chaos coming, as well as major economic problems. You are looking at some very powerful changes; be aware of that."[4]

Navajo and Hopi Prophecies

Hopi prophecies of the future are probably the most widely known and studied by those concerned about the apocalyptic events of the last days. The Navajo name for the Hopi, or Anasazi, means "ancient enemies."[5] This meaning may be because the Navajo have the X haplogroup that ties them to Israel, making them a likely offshoot of the Nephite and Lamanite populations. It's possible that they were those who were led away to preserve them from destruction, and the Hopi were of a kind who worshipped another God. The DNA haplogroup X noted among the Navajo at 7 percent suggests distant ties to the Nephite civilization. Archaeologists suggest that while most of those carrying the X haplogroup remained in the northeast among the Algonquians and Iroquois (who carried the haplogroup X at 15–25 percent), a branch moved west during the time the main stock was already well established in the east, where they evolved into what today are the Navajo. However, today they are a mix of many bloods, including Athabascan. By studying the position of the X haplogroup found among Native Americans on the genetic tree, it was discovered that an early split took place at the very beginning of the expansion and spread from the Near East. It seems that one complete Native American X sequence was found among the southwestern Navajo, and the other among the tribes in Ontario, who developed into the Ojibway over the centuries. The two sequences are believed to have diverged from a common point of origin after their common ancestor was already settled in America.[6]

The Navajo believe in both a good god and a bad god. The main use of their good god is to protect them from their evil one.[7] The Navajo's outlook for the future mimics the end-time prophecies of many of their distant Algonquian and Iroquois cousins. Not so with the Hopi, who preach only of death for those that don't fall in line with the teachings of their god Masauwu.

Navajo View of the End-Times

The end-time prophecies of the Navaho come in the form of chants. The *Unity Chant* speaks of the coming of a new religion, and of a new prophet of God who comes like the dawn and like the Shepherd who gathers his flock and brings all the wandering sheep back together again.[8] (This sounds like the emergence of the Prophet Joseph Smith and his role in the Restoration of the true Church of Jesus Christ; as well as the latter-day gathering of Israel from the corners of the earth back into the fold of Christ.)

> In the Day of Unity you will walk in beauty; the beauty will walk before you; you will be surrounded by beauty. Through the beautiful teachings of a new Prophet of God, these meanings will become very clear. Man himself in this Age has found many ways to create beauty. With these beautiful things we must now have beautiful minds. With beautiful minds we will have beautiful hearts. With beautiful hearts we will talk in beauty. The speech of all men will be in beauty. . . . Those who speak with beautiful speech will lead the world to beauty. . . . The center of this beautiful speech comes from a Holy Mountain.[9]

The Holy Mountain we can easily take to be the mountain of the Lord's house in the tops of the Rocky Mountains. Thousands of people come each year to this place to learn of God's holy ways and beautiful speech. This is a temple which will no doubt remain all though the Millennium:

> 2 And it shall come to pass in the last days, that the mountain of the Lord's house shall be established in the top of the mountains, and shall be exalted above the hills; and all nations shall flow unto it.
>
> 3 And many people shall go and say, Come ye, and let us go up to the mountain of the Lord, to the house of the God of Jacob; and he will teach us of his ways, and we will walk in his paths: for out of Zion shall go forth the law, and the word of the Lord from Jerusalem. (Isaiah 2:2–3)

Hopi Prophecies

Hopi prophecies are not so uplifting. From various versions of Hopi traditions, we learn that the earth god Masauwu told the Hopi to protect his world and to watch for the return of Pahana (the lost White Brother), who will be coming from the east. The Hopi maintain that their ancestors were led to this continent by a great chieftain who ultimately fell into wicked ways. His two sons scolded him, and after he died they took over the role of leadership. Masauwu gave each brother a set of tablets called Tiponi. Both were instructed to carry them to a place the sun god would direct them. The elder brother was told to go to the east toward the rising sun and, once reaching his destination, was to return and look for his younger brother who remained on the Turtle Islands (the name the Natives have for America). It is said that after so many years the elder brother (Pahana) may have changed the color of his skin, but that his hair will remain black. When he returns and finds his younger brother, their Tiponi tablets will be placed side by side to show the entire world that they are true brothers.[10]

The Great Day of Purification

The Hopi believe that the arrival of Pahana will signal the ushering in of the Fifth Age of the world, a time when these two brothers will help bring to pass the Great Day of Purification; a day when all the evildoers will either be punished or destroyed, and all the land that was taken from the younger brother will be restored. During the prophesied Great Day of Purification, the forces of the Swastika and the Sun (plus a third force symbolized by the color red—Red Russia or China?) will culminate in either a total rebirth or total annihilation of the world.[11]

The Return of Pahana

The true Pahana appears to be the earlier lost White Brother of the Hopi.[12] It is said the transformed elder brother (the True White Brother) will be wearing a red cloak or a red cap when he comes. He will bring no religion but his own. It is said that he will be so powerful that none will able to stand against him, and in one day he will gain control of this entire continent. It is also said that this "red force" will purify the Hopi people and unite all the major religions of the world into one world of universal brotherhood. Once the two brothers are united, the True White Brother will then open up the Tiponi tablets that Masauwu gave them and reveal the secret knowledge hidden within.[13]

The True White Brother of the Hopi

The Hopi initially thought Pahana might be among the Spanish conquistadors who arrived in AD 1519, the same time they expected the return of the Plumed Serpent, or Quetzalcoatl. But after the Hopi put the conquistadors through a series of tests, the Spaniards failed, and the Hopi sent them on their way. The Catholics and the Mormons were also put to the test once they entered Hopi lands, but they too failed the test and were sent away. Because the Hopi are said to have been led to the mesas by one to three men dressed in white robes, some have wondered if perhaps they were one or more of the three Nephites. But a quick look at their end-time prophecies clears that issue up. Hopi elders were reportedly told to sever the head of anyone who did not follow the true teachings of Masauwu during the Great Day of Purification—similar to the beheadings of Christians by some Muslims. In one description of the Tiponi tablets, a figure is drawn on the stone without a head, and a corner of the stone is broken off. Masauwu is said to have told the Hopi that when Pahana returns he will bring with him the broken-off corner, but if, in the meantime, a Hopi leader accepts a false religion, "he must assent to having his head cut off" as drawn on the stone.[14] Not something one would expect of the benevolent god of the universe and His loving son Jesus Christ. The once again speaks volumes about the identity of the god, Masauwu, also known as Skeletal Man, the Spirit of Death, the Earth God, and the door keeper of the Fifth World.[15]

The Hopi language is tied linguistically to the Uto-Aztecan language family, with the Aztecs being one of the most bloodthirsty civilizations ever to have lived. They were no doubt under the corrupting influence of Satan (described as the god of this world in the Bible). In 2 Corinthians, we read:

> 3 But if our gospel be hid, it is hid to them that are lost:
>
> 4 In whom the *god of this world* hath blinded the minds of them which believe not, lest the light of the glorious gospel of Christ, who is the image of God, should shine unto them.
>
> 5 For we preach not ourselves, but Christ Jesus the Lord; and ourselves your servants for Jesus' sake. (2 Corinthians 4:3–5; emphasis added)

The Nahuas, Toltecs, and Aztecs are generally all of one family of tribes and are tied by blood to Zarah-Judah and the seafaring Tribe of Dan. Dan was the first in Israel to take up to idol worship. Idol-worshipers were prime candidates for Satan to use as he pleased. The snake (or *naga*) cult of Hinduism and its close resemblance to the snake cults of the Hopi, also tie them to Dan (whose symbol is the serpent), and whose maritime explorations took them in India. It is said that two helpers will accompany the True White Brother. One helper will have the sign of a swastika (a masculine symbol of purity), and the other will have the sign of a Celtic cross with red lines (representing female life-blood).[16] Both can be tied to the Tuatha de Danann of Ireland. A people whose Danite and Scythian bloodline produced the Celts, and whose mother goddess Danu led her children on.

Who Is Pahana?

The identity of Pahana has long been a mystery. Yet modern researchers tend to tie him to someone in the Far East, usually in India or Tibet. Some have even tied him to Padmasambhava, also known as Guru Rinpoche, an eighth-century Indian Buddhist Master who is widely accepted as a second Buddha in Tibet, Nepal, Bhutan, and India. His traditional dress consisted of a red robe over his other layers, a blue tunic and a red monastic shawl.[17] The Guru Padmasambhava is said to hold a treasury of secret knowledge—a source of blessings and learning for all that has been kept secret among the Tibetans for generations. Much of that wisdom is said to be kept on a secret tablet similar to the Hopi Tiponi whose prophecies say that when "the iron bird flies,"[18] the red-robed people of the east will appear and the two brothers from across the great oceans will finally be reunited after their long separation. Some have even wondered if the two brothers have already come together. In *From the Roof of the World of the Land of Enchantment: The Tibet-Pueblo Connection* we read the following, "In the incongruous atmosphere of the Wilshire Hotel in Los Angeles, an extraordinary encounter took place in 1979. During the Dalai Lama's first visit to North America, he met with three Hopi elders. The spiritual leaders agreed to speak in only in their Native tongues. Through Hopi elder and interpreter Thomas Benyakya, delegation head Grandfather David's first words to the Dalai Lama were: 'Welcome home.'"[19]

Hindu Terrorists

Since September 11, 2001, the world attention has been focused chiefly on radical Muslim attacks and terror, but terrorists are also rising in India among the Hindus in their efforts to make Hinduism the national religion of India. These anti-Christian attacks include the murder of missionaries and priests, sexual assault on nuns, the destruction or ransacking of churches and convents, desecration of Christian cemeteries, and Bible burnings. In the past decade alone, Hindu extremists have increased their attacks on Christians, until there are now several hundred per year in their efforts to make sure that the Hindu religion remains the dominant religion throughout India and in their political system. Past attacks have been nonrandom mob violence, not triggered by some real or imagined insult, but rather, have been carefully planned attacks by organized Hindu extremists. They usually have an explicit program and a developed religious-nationalist ideology. Their idea is to drive all Muslims and Christians out.

The Hopi believe their people will play a pivotal role in the survival of the human race because of their vital communication and unseen powers that hold nature in balance. After the Hopi have fulfilled their pattern of life, Masauwu will be the leader, and only the Hopi brothers and sisters living in the Four Corners area will survive to begin a new way of life.

The Hopi maintain that besides the two Tiponi tablets, three other tablets exist. One tablet outlines the Hopi Empire, and is still in the hands of the chiefs of the Oraibi and Hotevilla pueblos in Arizona.[20]

> These were given to the Bear Clan by their patron deity Söqömhonaw, and essentially constituted a divine title to the lands where the Hopi settled after their migrations. The Hopi had a Universal Snake Dance. The third of these was etched with designs including the sun, moon, stars, clouds, etc. on one side with six human figures on the other. . . .
>
> A letter from the Hopi to the President of the United States in 1949 also declared that "the Stone Tablets, upon which are written the boundaries of the Hopi empire, are still in the hands of the Chiefs of Oraibi and Hotevilla pueblos"[21]

Hopi Nine Signs of the End-Times

The nine signs leading up to the Great Purification are as follows:

1. The Hopi see the *first sign* as the "coming of the white-skinned men . . . who struck their enemies with thunder" (White men with guns).
2. The *second sign* arrives with the coming of "spinning wheels filled with voices" (some say covered wagons filled with people).
3. The *third sign* signaled the coming of a "strange beast like a buffalo but with great long horns" that will "overrun the land in large numbers" (long-horned cattle).
4. The *fourth sign* is the crossing of the land "by snakes of iron" (railroads).
5. The *fifth sign* is the arrival of a giant spider web that

will crisscross the land (telephone and the Internet).

6. The *sixth sign* is the land being crisscrossed with "rivers of stone that make pictures in the sun" (highways).
7. The *seventh sign* will be when we hear of the "sea turning black, and many living things dying because of it" (oil spills).
8. The *eighth sign* arrives when you see "many youth, who wear their hair long" come and "join the tribal nations, to learn their ways and wisdom" (hippie movement of 1960s).
9. The *ninth, and final, sign* is described as a "dwelling-place in the heavens . . . that shall fall with a great crash. It will appear as a blue star." (It is reported that the ninth sign was the US Space Skylab, which fell to the Earth in 1979. "According to Australian eye-witnesses, it appeared to be burning blue."[22]

It is said that once these signs come to pass, there will be much for man to rebuild, with the return of Pahana taking place soon after. He will bring with him the dawn of the Fifth World. It is believed that we are now living in the Fourth World, and will enter the Fifth World after the Great Purification.

Moving On to Those in the North

As interesting as the foreboding end-time prophecies of the Hopi are, it will be from the northern Algonquians, Iroquois, and Cherokee that we find prophecies more in line with the prophecies given to the Nephites during their long stay in the promised land.

Notes

1. Sun Bear with Wabun Wind, *Black Dawn, Bright Day: Indian Prophecies for the Millennium That Reveal the Fate of the Earth* (New York: Simon & Schuster, 1992), 6.
2. John McIntosh, *The Origin of North American Indians; with a Faithful Description of Their Manners and Customs, Both Civil and Military, Their Religions, Languages, Dress, and Ornaments . . . .* (New York: Nafish & Cornish, 1849), 275–76.
3. Sun Bear with Wabun Wind, *Black Dawn, Bright Day: Indian Prophecies for the Millennium That Reveal the Fate of the Earth* (New York: Simon & Schuster, 1992), 29–30.
4. Ibid., 18.
5. Gayle Redfern, *Ancient Wisdoms: Exploring the Mysteries and Connections* (Bloomington, IN: AuthorHouse, 2009), 64.
6. Maere Reidla et al., "Origin and Diffusion of mtDNA Haplogroup X," *American Journal of Human Genetics* 75, no. 5, (November 2003), www.ncbi.nlm.nih.gov/pmc/articles/PMC1180497/.
7. Hubert Howe Bancroft, *The Works of Hubert Howe Bancroft: The Native Races* (San Francisco: A. L. Bancroft and Company, 1883), 3:171.
8. "Interpretation of Ancient Navajo Chants," Annie Khan, *Prophecy Fulfilled*, accessed March 24, 2017, prophecy-fulfilled .com/navajo.htm.
9. "Observations from the Navajo Nation," britjas, *LDS Freedom Forum*, accessed March 8, 2016, www.ldsfreedomforum.com /viewtopic.php?t=9492.
10. "Hopi Prophecy," in Frank Waters, *Book of the Hopi* (New York: Penguin Books, 1977), 408. Found online at www.welcomehome .org/rainbow/prophecy/hopi1.html.
11. "Hopi Prophecies," *Crystalinks*, accessed March 24, 2017, www .crystalinks.com/hopi2.html.
12. *Wikipedia*, s.v. "Hopi mythology," last modified March 9, 2017, en.wikipedia.org/wiki/Hopi_mythology.

13. Ibid.
14. Ibid.
15. Ibid.
16. Frank Waters, *Book of the Hopi* (New York: Penguin Books, 1977), 408. Quoted in "Hopi Prophecy,| *Welcome Home*, accessed March 20, 2017, www.welcomehome.org/rainbow/prophecy /hopi1.html.
17. *Wikipedia*, s.v. "Padmasambhava," last modified November 23, 2016, en.wikipedia.org/wiki/Padmasambhava.
18. "Tibet, Tibet," *Martine & Stephen Batchelor*, accessed March 25, 2017, www.stephenbatchelor.org/index.php/en/tibet-tibet.
19. Antonio Lopez, *From the Roof of the World to the Land of Enchantment: The Tibet-Pueblo Connection* in "Links/Similiarities between Tibetan and Native America Groups," Tibet Diary, *Tibetalk*, accessed March 20, 2017, tibettalk.wordpress.com/2007/11/01 /linkssimilarities-between-tibetan-and-native-american-groups/.
20. Frank Waters, *Book of the Hopi* (New York: Penguin Books, 1977), 408. Quoted in "Hopi Prophecy,| *Welcome Home*, accessed March 20, 2017, www.welcomehome.org/rainbow/prophecy /hopi1.html.
21. Wikipedians, ed., *Mythologies: A Polytheistic View of the World* (PediaPress), 454–55.
22. Frank Waters, *Book of the Hopi* (New York: Penguin Books, 1977), 408. Quoted in "Hopi Prophecy,| *Welcome Home*, accessed March 20, 2017, www.welcomehome.org/rainbow/prophecy /hopi1.html.

10

The Iroquois Prophets

As noted in chapter four, archaeologists maintain that the New York Iroquois evolved right there in New York from the people of the Point Peninsula culture who arrived in western New York around 600 BC. They were a people that evidence suggests were the Nephites.[1] Not surprisingly, and of major importance in determining Book of Mormon territory, the Five Nations of the Iroquois have always maintained that the ground their people walked on in New York was their ancestral domain.[2] Through conquest and migration, the Iroquois gained control of most of the northeastern United States and of eastern Canada; however, for the most part they remained in their upstate New York villages.

Samuel the Lamanite Prophet

As wild as the Iroquois have been described as being, there were a great many among them that were righteous. There were also prophets among them, just like there had been during their ancestral past. The Book of Mormon's Samuel the Lamanite prophet, for instance, was sent to call the wayward Nephites to repentance by the Lord around 5 BC. The Nephites were steeped in wickedness at this time, while the Lamanites were keeping the commandments in strict accordance to the law of Moses (see Helaman 13:1). Samuel managed to teach the people of Zarahemla for several days, but was eventually cast out of the city. However, the Lord had a message for these wayward Nephites. He told Samuel to return to Zarahemla and tell them that doom lay ahead for them if they did not repent and return to the God of their ancient Israelite fathers. Unfortunately, Samuel was not even allowed entrance into the city this time. Thus, he simply climbed to the top of the city wall, raised his arms, and said,

> 5 Behold, I, Samuel, a Lamanite, do speak the words of the Lord which he doth put into my heart; and behold he hath put it into my heart to say unto this people that the sword of justice hangeth over this people; and four hundred years pass not away save the sword of justice falleth upon this people.
>
> 6 Yea, heavy destruction awaiteth this people, and it surely cometh unto this people, and nothing can save this people save it be repentance and faith on the Lord Jesus Christ, who surely shall come into the world, and shall suffer many things and shall be slain for his people.
>
> 7 And behold, an angel of the Lord hath declared it unto me, and he did bring glad tidings to my soul. And behold, I was sent unto you to declare it unto you also, that ye might have glad tidings; but behold ye would not receive me.
>
> 8 Therefore, thus saith the Lord: Because of the hardness of the hearts of the people of the Nephites, except they repent I will take away my word from them, and I will withdraw my Spirit from them, and I will suffer them no longer, and I will turn the hearts of their brethren against them. . . .
>
> 10 Yea, I will visit them in my fierce anger, and there shall be those of the fourth generation who shall live, of your enemies, to behold your utter destruction; and this shall surely come except ye repent, saith the Lord; and those of the fourth generation shall visit your destruction.
>
> 11 But if ye will repent and return unto the Lord your God I will turn away mine anger, saith the Lord; yea, thus saith the Lord, blessed are they who will repent and turn unto me, but wo unto him that repenteth not. (Helaman 13:5–8, 10–11)

Unfortunately, not only was his message rejected, but the people of Zarahemla even tried to kill him by casting stones and shooting arrows at him, none of which could hit their mark, for Samuel was protected by divine intervention.

The American British War

Today, the Iroquois still exist in New York as a distinct people living under their own tribal laws and nominally recognized by the

US government as an independent nation. In 1779, during the American British War, the Iroquois fought on the side of the British, which caused major reprisals by American troops because they were intent on destroying anything that contributed to the British. As a result, forty towns were destroyed, along with their corn crops and orchards, leaving hardly a food plant to sustain the Iroquois throughout the coming winter. The tribes even divided against each other because of their hardships and political views, and some moved north into Ontario among other members of their people. As one author wrote, "The story of how they have preserved themselves through three centuries of contact with an invading race that had little love for them and whose policy like their own in ancient times, is to absorb or exterminate, to accomplish a thing that no other aboriginal race has done, is well worth a place in history as one of its marvels."[3]

Iroquois Territory

The Iroquois were spread all across western and central New York during the early years of European colonization. The Onondaga branch of the Iroquois were considered the easternmost branch of the Iroquois tribes. They occupied much of the area around Lake Onondaga at the east end of the Finger Lakes region near Albany, New York. The Cayuga and Seneca branches of the Iroquois lived to the west of them, just off the coast of Lake Erie in western New York. The Oneida and Mohawks lived just to the east of them. The tribes traditionally met together at Lake Onondaga where a long line of prophets by that name had lived, and just as their traditional chiefs do today, with the Onondaga considered the "*Keepers of the Fire*."

The Iroquois Prophet Onandagus

The Prophet Onandagus was likely an Iroquois. He was a man of God noted in the story of the white Lamanite Zelph. His bones were found in a burial mound in Illinois by Joseph Smith and the men who joined him on their march from Ohio to Zion's Camp. After the Prophet Joseph Smith prayed for answers to the identity of the man whose bones they had found, he was informed that the bones were the remains of a white Lamanite named Zelph. Zelph was a man of God and a warrior chief under the great Prophet Onandagus who was known from the Hill Cumorah to the Rocky Mountains.[4]

The Iroquois Prophet Handsome Lake

Because of their sheer numbers and their skills as warriors, both the Iroquois and the Algonquians were considered formidable enemies when the white Europeans first began to colonize the land. Their large settlements, which ranged from small hamlets to villages of several hundred people, were large enough to ward off the white man's advances in spite of his superior weapons. However, there were some weapons the Indians could not hide from, nor even defend themselves against: disease and hard liquor. Yet, while white man's drink was deadly for the Indians, in one instance it brought about the reformation of not only the man Handsome Lake, but his entire nation.

> Handsome Lake Movement, also called Longhouse Religion or Gai'Wiio . . . is the longest-established prophet movement in North America. Its founder was Ganioda'yo, a Seneca chief whose name meant "Handsome Lake"; his trance revelations in 1799 transformed the demoralized Seneca. Their Christian beliefs included a personal creator-ruler, a devil, heaven, hell, and judgment; Jesus was identified with a local mythological figure. Seneca divinities were retained as ruling angels, rituals were reduced to four transformed dance feasts, and the longhouse was modified into a "church." A puritan and modernizing ethic attacked alcohol and witchcraft, banned further land sales, encouraged the men to practice plow agriculture and animal husbandry, and stressed stability of the nuclear family.[5]

The Story of Handsome Lake

The story of Handsome Lake, a Seneca Iroquois, is a story of conversion, repentance, and hope. He was born along New York's Genesee River in 1735—the Iroquois' ancestral homeland. He was described as being a mature man of average stature who was hopelessly addicted to white man's "fire-water." In fact, many of his people were struggling with the same addiction and found themselves unable to manage their everyday affairs, let alone worry about their futures. Handsome Lake ultimately became so sick that he lay like a helpless invalid in the home of his daughter and her husband for several years. His unspecified illness was totally debilitating and was no doubt aggravated by his use of hard liquor. He knew this, but could not seem to stop.

Handsome Lake's addiction left him riddled with guilt and made him feel completely worthless before the Great Spirit his people worshipped. Even so, he thought of the Great Spirit often when the sunlight poured into his room each morning, because he knew it was the Creator who had provided the light and warmth. When he heard the birds singing each day, he thanked the Great Ruler of heaven and earth for their music. As he looked up at night and saw the stars, he knew that the Great Ruler had created them and was thankful. Thus, one night he implored the Great Father of the sky world to let him live, for he had been wasting away to skin and bones during his four long years of confinement and was not sure he could make it through even one more day.

One morning, Handsome Lake's daughter heard her father cry out. Startled, she looked up just in time to see her father staggering toward her, completely out of control. Immediately, she rushed to catch him, but he fell dying at her feet. She and her husband carried him inside, dressed him for burial, and sent for their relatives to say their last goodbyes. Strangely, those who were mourning him noticed that part of his body was still warm, suggesting that he was just in a coma, not dead. They held off burying him and were grateful to have waited, for in three days Handsome Lake awoke from his deep sleep and exclaimed that he had been to the sky world and had conversed with the Redeemer. This story is similar to the story of the spiritually induced coma of the Lamanite king Lamoni in the Book of Mormon. Lamoni was totally overcome by the Spirit after hearing the glad news of the gospel.

The Lamanite King Lamoni's Visionary Experience

The story of King Lamoni's visionary experience proved to the Lamanites that the Christ that the Nephites had been teaching them about would surely come. From Alma we read the following,

> 41 And he began to cry unto the Lord, saying: O Lord, have mercy; according to thy abundant mercy which thou hast had upon the people of Nephi, have upon me, and my people.
>
> 42 And now, when he had said this, he fell unto the earth, as if he were dead.
>
> 43 And it came to pass that his servants took him and carried him in unto his wife, and laid him upon a bed; and he lay as if he were dead for

> the space of two days and two nights; and his wife, and his sons, and his daughters mourned over him, after the manner of the Lamanites, greatly lamenting his loss. (Alma 18:40–43)

In the next chapter we read,

> 1 And it came to pass that after two days and two nights they were about to take his body and lay it in a sepulchre, which they had made for the purpose of burying their dead. . . .
>
> 12 And it came to pass that he arose, according to the words of Ammon; and as he arose, he stretched forth his hand unto the woman, and said: Blessed be the name of God, and blessed art thou.
>
> 13 For as sure as thou livest, behold, I have seen my Redeemer; and he shall come forth, and be born of a woman, and he shall redeem all mankind who believe on his name. Now, when he had said these words, his heart was swollen within him, and he sunk again with joy; and the queen also sunk down, being overpowered by the Spirit (Alma 19:1, 12–13)

Handsome Lake's Visionary Experience

Like King Lamoni, once Handsome Lake awoke from his coma, he reported that he had been to the upper world where he met four beings, one of which was the Savior who guided him through a series of visionary experiences. Handsome Lake was then told to take his visionary experiences back to the earth world and teach his people. As Handsome Lake began his recital of his exciting visionary experiences, he explained that three holy men had bid him welcome when he arrived in the upper world. They said that a fourth had gone to report his arrival, but would shortly return. He described the three messengers as being dressed in fine raiment and that they were very handsome and commanding men. He explained that these three holy men had a message for him from the Creator (who was very much aware of Handsome Lake's sad condition and his thankful heart), and bid the three messengers visit him and help him recover. That help came in the form of berries, which the messengers said, once prepared for him by his people would make him well.

Handsome Lake's Journey Along the Sky Road

As Handsome Lake's story proceeds, he explained that while wrapped in vision, the three messengers led him along the great sky-road that led to the abode of the Creator. Unlike the Hopi, who claimed that those who ventured into the underworld and saw their god Masauwu would be frozen in fear, Handsome Lake noted the most marvelous and beautiful things along the sky road, including delicious looking fruits growing on the wayside. He even noted smelling the "fragrant odors of the flowers along the road," and that every kind of bird flew in the sky above.[6]

Meeting the Fourth Messenger

This great sky road ultimately led them to the sky world itself where they were destined to meet the fourth messenger. Once they arrived, the messengers told Handsome Lake that they would show him many things, including the works of those living on earth, the house of the punisher, and the lands of the Creator Himself.[7]

Just as promised, Handsome Lake was greeted by the spirit of a relative as they journeyed along, and even a dog he remembered. He saw the fate of the righteous, and the fate of the wicked (who were held captive by the wicked one, which Handsome Lake described as a frightful demon). Yet, as grand as all this was, meeting the fourth messenger was to be the grandest of all, for it was none other than the Savior himself.

As the vision of the Master opened, the Master was walking along the road toward Handsome Lake and the other messengers, but then he passed them. Once a fair distance apart, the messengers and Handsome Lake turned to look at him and saw that he was looking back at them, and thus, they greeted each other.

The fourth messenger then asked Handsome Lake a question: "*Did you never hear your grandfathers say that once there was a certain man upon the earth across the great waters who was slain by his own people*?" Handsome Lake answered in the affirmative, at which point the fourth messenger said: "*I am he*," (Segan'hedûs—He who resurrects).[8]

The fourth messenger then showed Handsome Lake the scars on his hands and feet that had the appearance of being torn by iron nails, and the scar on his side created by a spear. This was the same thing Christ did to identify Himself when He appeared to Handsome Lake's ancient fathers during His visit to the Nephites after His death and Resurrection. The fourth messenger then said, "They slew me because of their independence and unbelief. So I have gone home to shut the doors of heaven that they may not see me again until the earth passes away.

Then will all the people cry to me for succor, and when I come it will be in this wise: my face will be sober and I shall turn it to my people."[9]

Handsome Lake's Return

After giving Handsome Lake a series of social, political, and spiritual instructions for himself and his people, the messengers told them that it was time for them to part because it was the intentions of the Great Spirit that Handsome Lake return and teach his people the things he had learned. First and foremost, he was to teach that the Creator made every living creature, and that he and he alone should be worshipped. Among the things the Creator forbade, four were of particular importance and must be stopped immediately:

1. Drinking hard liquor, which incapacitated his people.[10]
2. The use of witchcraft, which the Iroquois say was introduced to them by others.[11]
3. The use of charms and amulets.[12]
4. Abortion.[13]

The Creator said that anyone who indulged in such offenses were in need of sore repentance.

Handsome Lake as a Missionary

After Handsome Lake returned to the land of the living, he spent the next sixteen years teaching what is referred to as "*Gai'Wiio,*" to his countrymen. His prophetic mission made a major impact on his Iroquois brothers, although not without a struggle by certain dissenters, especially Corn Planter, his brother. But, in time, the old ways of the Iroquois were done away with. They are now simply referred to as their Old Testament, and the new religion is called their Long House religion. The philosophy, or religion, referred to as Gai'Wiio, is much like the code of all Christian nations. They were taught that they should not intermarry or be abusive to their spouses or children. They were taught the evils of card playing and intemperance—the punishment for each was graphically described. They were taught to not be stingy, to not bare false witness against their neighbors, to not steal, to not borrow without returning, to not be prideful or boast of the things the Creator had blessed them with—many of the same things taught by the Savior to his Nephite ancestors. The code went on and on, imparting wisdom and council about everything from family matters to social and political matters. It laid out a system whereby they might live in favor with both God and man. The code also included a series of prophecies that culminate with the destruction of the wicked and the preservation of the righteous who live the good message and the laws of peace given them by the Lord Jesus Christ.

The Prophecies of the Three Messengers

1. "We, the messengers of the Creator, are of the opinion that the world will continue for three generations longer."[14] "Handsome Lake taught that the world would end in 2100."[15]
2. "There will be a time when all the earth will withhold its sustaining foods. Then will come the end of the world when those who refuse to believe in Gai'wiio [Good Message], will suffer great hardships."[16]
3. "Now we think that a time will come when a great plague will kill man[y] people and no one will know its cause. Then will you know that the end is near and those who do not believe will suffer great hardships."[17]
4. "In that time every poisonous creature will appear. These creatures the Creator has imprisoned in the underworld and they are the creations of the evil-minded spirit. Now it is our opinion that when they are released many people will be captured and poisoned by them. Men will see these hardships when they fail to believe in Gai'wiio."[18]
5. "Now we think when the end comes the earth will be destroyed by fire and not one upon it will escape for all the earth will be enveloped in flames and all those who refuse to believe in Gai'wiio will be in it."[19]

The instruction and prophecies continued through 130 sections, each addressing a different aspect of the Iroquois' lives. Handsome Lake spent the rest of his life imparting this code of law to his countrymen with more than modest success.

Handsome Lake's Mission Ends

After being invited to preach in Onondaga in central New York, Handsome Lake had a vision telling him that if he went, he would be singing his death song, but that he should go anyway because his countrymen at Onondaga were stretching out their hands pleading for him to come.[20] It is said that quite a group went with Handsome Lake to Onondaga, which brought the aging prophet great comfort.

After arriving at Onondaga and preaching to a few followers, Handsome Lake predicted his own death and spoke of seeing a pathway covered with grass in vision. He said: "I will soon go to my new home. Soon I step into the new world for there is a plain pathway before me leading there."[21] He then retired to his cabin, and after a distressing illness, commenced his walk over the path he saw in a vision. Handsome Lake had finally gone home to the sky world of his fathers, and to the Creator of us all.

> Note: The interesting story of Handsome Lake can be found in Arthur C. Parker's account of the Code of Handsome Lake, the Seneca Prophet, which he put together in 1913.

Notes

1. Phyllis Carol Olive, *The Lost Lands of the Book of Mormon* (Springville, UT: Cedar Fort, 2012).
2. "Handsome Lake Religion," in Arthur C. Parker, "The Code of Handsome Lake, the Seneca Prophet," *Internet Sacred Text Archive*, accessed March 20, 2017, www.sacred-texts.com/nam/iro/parker/index.htm.
3. "Section 44," in Parker, "The Code of Handsome Lake, the Seneca Prophet."
4. "Zelph Revisited," Donald Q. Cannon, accessed March 20, 2017, emp.byu.edu/marrottr/341folder/zelph%20%revisit%20cannon.html. See also "Zelph Revisited," in "Documents List," emp.byu.edu/marrottr/DocuList.htm. See also Kenneth W. Godfrey, "What Is the Significance of Zelph in the Study of Book of Mormon Geography?," *Journal of Book of Mormon Studies* 8, no. 2 (1999), 70–79.

5. *Britannica Encyclopedia of World Religions*, s.v. "Handsome Lake Movement." For more information see, "The Code of Handsome Lake, the Seneca Prophet," Arthur C. Parker, *Internet Sacred Text Archive*, accessed March 20, 2017, www.sacred-texts.com/nam/iro/parker/index.htm.
6. "Section 112," in Parker, "The Code of Handsome Lake, the Seneca Prophet."
7. "Section 82," in Parker, "The Code of Handsome Lake, the Seneca Prophet."
8. "Section 94," in Parker, "The Code of Handsome Lake, the Seneca Prophet."
9. Ibid.
10. "Section 50," in Parker, "The Code of Handsome Lake, the Seneca Prophet."
11. "Section 72," in Parker, "The Code of Handsome Lake, the Seneca Prophet."
12. "Section 3," in Parker, "The Code of Handsome Lake, the Seneca Prophet."
13. "Section 4," in Parker, "The Code of Handsome Lake, the Seneca Prophet."
14. "Section 39," in Parker, "The Code of Handsome Lake, the Seneca Prophet."
15. Ibid., fn. 1.
16. "Section 40," in Parker, "The Code of Handsome Lake, the Seneca Prophet."
17. "Section 71," in Parker, "The Code of Handsome Lake, the Seneca Prophet."
18. "Section 74," in Parker, "The Code of Handsome Lake, the Seneca Prophet."
19. "Section 77," in Parker, "The Code of Handsome Lake, the Seneca Prophet."
20. "Section 122," in Parker, "The Code of Handsome Lake, the Seneca Prophet."
21. "Section 130," in Parker, "The Code of Handsome Lake, the Seneca Prophet."

11

Cherokee Prophecies

The Iroquois weren't the only descendants of the seed of Lehi that were privileged to special attention from heaven because God was ever mindful of Lehi's children of the forest. The Cherokees were also in need of help now that new white immigrants had begun to spread across the land. Thus, just as He had done with the Anishinaabe living along the Atlantic coast (they had been warned to moved farther inland to protect them from destruction by early European colonizers), He gave the Cherokee who were living in the Great Smoky Mountains between North Carolina and Tennessee a prophetic warning. The Cherokee say that during a period of feuding and warfare between their own people, seven of their most holy men met around a great fire to ask God for guidance. For the next seven days, each of the medicine men in turn climbed to the top of a nearby mountain to pray and ask God what the future held for them. On the seventh day, they saw a light brighter than day appear over them, and heard a voice that said,

> I am a messenger from God. God has heard your prayers and He has great passion for your people and from now on you shall be called Keetoowah. Go back to your fire and worship. There is a white ball from way east, who is your enemy, coming and your grandchildren's feet are directed west. They shall have great trials on the edge of the prairie. They shall be divided into different factions and their blood shall be only [one] half. Families shall be divided against each other and they shall disregard their chiefs, leaders, medicine men, and captains. But if these younger generations should endeavor to follow God's instructions

there is a chance to turn back east, and if not, the next move shall be west, on the coast and from there on to the boat and this shall be the last."[1] (Three prophecies noted in this recital have already come to pass)

Once the messenger of God finished his prophecies of their future, the seven holy men went down from the mountain and told the people about the marvelous things they had learned.

Prophecy One

There is a white ball (the white Europeans) *from way east, who is your enemy, coming and your grandchildren's feet are directed west.*

This prophecy was fulfilled when warfare broke out in Cherokee country when foreign agents of France, England, and Spain were each vying for trade routes through Cherokee territory. This sent many of the Cherokee west across the Mississippi into the hills of Arkansas, Missouri, and Oklahoma in search of new homes to settle. Thus, the Cherokee became a divided people. Those in the west were formerly named the Western Cherokee Nation in the treaties of 1817, 1819, and 1833. Those in the east retained the name of the Keetoowah Cherokee. As foreign nations and early colonists continued to harass the eastern Cherokee (who were constantly receiving letters from their western loved ones who kept speaking of their fertile lands and happy circumstances), they too ultimately moved west and joined them in the hilly country of the Ozarks, which covers portions of Missouri, Arkansas, Oklahoma, and Kansas. However, the two divisions retained separate national identities. Unfortunately, not all of the tribes followed. Thus, in 1830, Andrew Jackson authorized the Indian Removal Act, and during the fall and winters of 1838 and 1839, the last of the Cherokee were forcibly moved west by the United States government. Four thousand Cherokee died on that long migration: a migration that has since become known as the Trail of Tears.[2] *Prophecy fulfilled!*

Prophecy Two

The Cherokee would be divided into different factions and their blood shall be only [one] half. The Cherokee found the hilly country of the Ozarks very much like the lands they left behind in the Great Smoky Mountains, and thus they put down roots. But once white settlers also began to settle the region, the Cherokee adopted much of the settlers' culture. The Cherokee began to intermarry with the settlers until their own culture was all but lost, and their blood was diluted by half, just as the messenger prophesied. *Prophecy fulfilled!*

Prophecy Three

Families shall be divided against each other and they shall disregard their chiefs, leaders, medicine men, and captains.

Just as prophesied, once the Cherokee adopted more and more of the white European culture, division among their own tribes occurred. The prophecy also included a time when their young people would disregard their wise men and tell them that what they said did not matter anymore. We see the fulfillment of that prophecy in our day, for Cherokee youth have left their reservations and have melted into the mainstream of America. They stand shoulder to shoulder with the children of the white man in their educational pursuits and choice of professions, which are different than the traditional ways of the fathers. *Prophecy fulfilled!*

Cherokee and Hebrew Ties

Those who study the Cherokee and document their customs, civil policies, history, language, religion, priests, military customs, agricultures, marriage ceremonies, funeral rites, and their temperaments and manners found them all to have close affinities with the customs and traits of the Hebrews. In fact, the cultural evidence of a Hebrew presence in the native North American tribes is so overwhelming that it can no longer be doubted that many Native Americans of northeastern America have ties that link them to the Near East and Israel. For some time, before the Iroquois took over New York (after the battle at Cumorah), New York seems to have been largely in control of the Algonquian tribes (Mulekite and Nephite populations). James Adair who spent many years among these people, noted their close ties to Hebrew's twelve tribes of Israel, including their affinity to divide into tribes. He tells us that,

> They tell one set of traditions which treat of the adventures of eight, ten, and sometimes twelve brothers. The youngest of these brothers is represented in many traditions which mention them, as the wisest and most beloved of their father, and lying under the special guardianship of the Great Spirit. In one tradition . . . he delivers his brethren from divers difficulties entailed on them from their own folly and disobedience. In another tradition he is made to supply his brethren with corn. . . . The

similarity between these and other traditions, with the Bible stories of Jacob and his twelve sons [the youngest of which is Joseph, the father of Lehi's Nephite and Lamanite children], cannot fail to attract the attention of any person who is acquainted with both versions.[3]

Both the Algonquians and Iroquois stem from the same patriarchal lines (the Cherokee are simply a southern branch of the Iroquois). The Cherokee see themselves as children of God. The God of the Cherokee is the Creator of all things, including the ability of men to choose their own path—the white path of peace. According to Cherokee oral traditions, the Cherokee spoke the name of Jesus long before his birth two thousand years ago. James Adair, in his *History of the American Indians*, speaks of deity as being the immediate head of their state, and that "*all the nations of Indians are exceedingly intoxicated with religious pride . . . because their supposed ancestors, as they affirm, were under the immediate government of the Deity who was present with them, in a very particular manner, and directed them by prophets.*"[4] Adair noted further that their religious rites, "which they derived from their illustrious predecessors,—strictly charging them not to deviate, in the least, out of that old, beloved, beaten path, and they will surely meet with all the success that attended their beloved forefathers."[5] He adds further, "The American Indians are so far from being Atheists, as some godless Europeans have flattered themselves, to excuse their own infidelity, that they have the great sacred name of God, that describes his divine essence, and by which he manifested himself to Moses—and are firmly persuaded they now live under the immediate government of Deity."[6]

The Cherokee claim that "Yohewah" [Jehovah] was the head of their state and that they had no other king before them. They, like the Hebrews, had an ark reminiscent of the ark of the covenant, which was carried on the back of a brave as they journeyed. According to the ecclesiastical year outlined by Moses, the Cherokee started their year at the first appearance of the new moon of the vernal equinox. Thus, although the law of Moses had been fulfilled with the coming of Christ, they nonetheless continued with what they could remember of the law. The Cherokee are often seen as being more civilized than any of the neighboring tribes.

The Cherokee Today

In response to the Gentile's efforts to take God out of every aspect of our lives, the Eastern Band of Cherokee have displayed the Ten Commandments in respect and devotion to God. The US Constitution does not apply to the Native Americans, who feel the need to honor and stand up for God in spite of the unbelief among the Gentiles. This is a practice that will earn them the blessings of the Almighty who will strengthen them in their righteous desires.

Cherokee End-Time Prophecies

Cherokee prophecies of the future were handed down from grandmother to grandchild long before the Europeans discovered Turtle Island (America). I've listed five of their prophecies below.

1. Each generation was warned of the arrival of the "monster with white eyes" (Europeans) from across the eastern sea who would have "terrifying power and would wreck destruction it its path."[7]
2. They were told that once they (the Europeans) arrived, the "spirits of the animals and trees [would begin] to wither," and the heartbeat of Mother Earth would become faint.[8]
3. Grandmothers told their grandchildren that things would become so harsh that the Earth would begin to sing its death song, and that when that happened many of the children of the white monster would rise up and "realize that they faced annihilation at the hands of their fathers."[9]
4. Around the same time, the spirit of the tribes would also be reborn, and would "guide the children of the white eyed-monster" in a joint effort to heal the Earth again.[10]
5. It was said that the "few keepers of the truth would emerge" and "become strong enough to overcome the power of the white-eyed monster." The children of the tribes would lead the people back to the right ways because the children of the forest had lived in harmony with the Earth for thousands of years and knew its heartbeat well.[11]

A Remnant of Jacob

Are the remnants of Jacob noted in the Book of Mormon among those who will become strong enough to overpower the white-eyed monster? This prophecy will crop up more than once in this book, for the seed of Lehi was given this land as an eternal inheritance. His Lamanite descendants are all that remain of those once great civilizations to witness the fulfillment of that promise.

> 15 And I say unto you, that if the Gentiles do not repent after the blessing which they shall receive, after they have scattered my people—[the Lamanites]
>
> 16 Then shall ye [the Lamanites], who are a remnant of the house of Jacob, go forth among them; and ye shall be in the midst of them who shall be many; and ye shall be among them as a lion among the beasts of the forest, and as a young lion among the flocks of sheep, who, if he goeth through both treadeth down and teareth in pieces, and none can deliver. (3 Nephi 20:15–16)

Notes

1. "Legend of the Keetoowah," Ken Martin, *Manataka American Indian Council*, accessed March 20, 2017, www.manataka.org/page275.html.
2. *Wikipedia*, s.v. "Indian Removal Act," last modified March 27, 2017, en.wikipedia.org/wiki/Indian_Removal_Act.
3. Samuel Cole Williams, *Adair's History of the American Indians* (New York: Promontory Press, 1986), 70.
4. Ibid., 34–35.
5. Ibid., 35.
6. Ibid., 37.
7. "Monster with the White-Eyes," in "Cherokee Prophecies," *Crystalinks*, accessed March 27, 2017, www.crystalinks.com/cherokeeprophecy.html.
8. Ibid.
9. Ibid.
10. Ibid.
11. Ibid.

12

The Prophecies of Deganawida

The Iroquois holy man Deganawida is best known in connection with Hiawatha in the formation of the Iroquois League of Nations. Yet, he also had some interesting prophecies of the future. In fact, his prophecies may well be the most comprehensive of those yet presented, taking us from the arrival of the white man to America through the turbulent end-times and on into the Millennium. Thus, his prophecy of the three warring serpents is well worth repeating for those of our day.

> AUTHOR'S NOTE: A variety of versions of the three-serpent prophecy has been given. Thus, I will simply try to paraphrase the versions given by a Tuscarora holy man—Wallace Mad Bear Anderson and Red Elk, whose versions are very similar. Both are cited in the endnotes.

The Three Warring Serpents

It is said that when Deganawida was leaving his people, he prophesied that they would one day "face a time of great suffering." A great *white serpent* would come upon the Iroquois. The serpent would be accepted as a friend, but would ultimately become so obsessed with power that it would attempt to choke the "life's blood out of the Indian people" if they did not succumb to it.[1]

> NOTE: The early US government did everything it could to destroy the Native Americans and free up their lands for the arrival of

more and more white colonists into eastern North America. Thus, this prophecy has been fulfilled.

The *white serpent* would slowly corrupt and separate the people. Eventually, the separation would be so bad that the family fire would be almost nonexistent. Deganawida warned: "If the family fire was ever allowed to be broken, if brother took to warfare against his brother, it would be only a matter of time before all was lost. A great despair would fall upon the People and the land. Since the People were the land it would be that in time [even] the land would start to die."[2]

The Red Serpent and the Onset of War

As the Deganawida Prophecy continues, we learn that the once proud Indians would become weary of the endless torment of the *white serpent*. Then, one day, a great *red serpent* would appear in the east, and a great battle would ensue between the two, a battle that would be so great that the whole earth would appear to shake, and this world-shaking event would occur three times.

> NOTE: Could this have reference to the First and Second World Wars, with a third war on the horizon for America? The Lord revealed to His prophets that the greatest threat to the United States is a vast worldwide secret combination. Ezra Taft Benson identified this worldwide secret combination as Communism, which would have to be destroyed before the Second Coming, in order to preserve the land of Zion. Joseph Smith also gave several prophetic warnings about the dangers of attacks from Communist countries, including China.[3]

Deganawida prophesied that the battle between the red and white serpents would seem to go on forever. After a time, the *white serpent* would momentarily give up, but would be struck by the *red serpent*, whose powers had mysteriously grown to great size. The *white serpent* would become so terrified that it would release the Indians, leaving the *white serpent* to devote all its attention to the *red serpent*.

> NOTE: George Albert Smith had a prophetic vision concerning a coming attack on America by Russia. An attack that he said would make World War II look like a training mission. He said that it would be terrible beyond belief because atomic missiles

would be unleashed against the United States, and people would die like flies.[4]

Fleeing to the West

The survivors would head west toward the *hilly country*, far from grasp of the *red serpent*. Hidden there in the *hilly country*, their wounds would heal and they would once again seek a more peaceful way of life, returning to ways that are more in harmony with Mother Earth. Deganawida saw streams of people (not just the Native Americans), heading for the land of the *hilly country* from all four directions, each looking for relief from the war and terror.[5]

Note: Could these streams of people be those who will ultimately make their way west to that part of the hilly country of the Ozarks, which lie in southern Missouri, not far from Jackson County [in western Missouri]? Will they meet up where the Saints of the Most High will have already begun the construction of the city of Zion—a place of refuge from the storms of the last days; a place where they can be nurtured and healed from the effects of the devastation going on in the rest of the country?

Note: The Cherokee Indians have a common belief that the Creator wished the Cherokee to stay west of the Mississippi, in order to remove themselves from European influences. Thus, they settled in what has been described as the *hilly* and mountainous areas of Arkansas, southern Missouri, eastern Oklahoma, southern Kansas, and northeastern Texas. Not surprisingly, and likely by heavenly design, the Western Cherokee are now living in close proximity to the place of the Lord's city of Zion, destined to be built in Jackson County, Missouri.

Lamanite Conversion

Deganawida prophesied that as the Indian people watched the battle going on between the *serpents*, that a great message would come and humble them. They would begin to watch for a young Indian boy who would become a *Choice Seer*. "Nobody knows who he is, or where he comes from, but he will be given Great Power," and will be accepted as their leader. It is said that he would instruct the Indians to refrain from going back to their homelands in the east, but to gather in the land of the *hilly country.*[6]

War Continues

As the Deganawida prophecy of the warring serpents continues, we find that once the Indians were safely settled in the *hilly country,* they would slowly lose the fear that was spreading across the country like a plague. As they continue to watch the *serpent war,* it seems like it would never end.[7]

The war caused a variety of problems.

- The mountains would crack open and spew fire.
- The rivers would boil.
- The fish would die.
- The trees would lose their leaves.
- No grass would grow.
- Strange bugs would crawl out of the ground and fall from the sky.
- Fire would come forth from the "Mother's Belly" and move across the land in great clouds of fire. Could this have reference to the eruption of the giant volcanic caldera at Yellowstone, or one of the other large volcanoes around the world?
- Death would be everywhere.[8]

The Arrival of the Black Serpent

Continuing on, we learn that one day, an Indian warrior would see the *red serpent* pluck a hair from the neck of the *white serpent.* This hair would be carried by the wind and found by a great *black serpent.* While the *black serpent* studied the white hair, the hair would turn into a white bird and then a white woman. She would tell him stories of death and horror.[9]

The Black Serpent Defeats the Red and White Serpents

The *black serpent* had become so infuriated at what he had learned that he let out a great roar that it could be felt around the earth and in the heavens. Then, the *black serpent* would enter the battle between the *red* and *white serpents* and defeat them. Now the *black serpent* would take on the evil of both serpents and become a power of darkness that defies description. It would appear that he had every intention of devouring the whole earth, and even the heavens in his fury.[10]

> NOTE: According to the interpretation the Chippewa medicine man, Sun Bear, the *white* and *red serpents* represent the United States and the Soviet Union. Two countries that would wrestle in a cold war until they were in so much debt that they couldn't afford to continue any longer. Sun Bear takes the *black serpent* to be the Muslim nations who have control of the world's oil supplies, and have succeeded in getting both the United States and Russia into wars they didn't know how to fight. In time, Sun Bear saw the United States and the Soviet Union enter a war with the Muslim nations; a war that is destined to affect all the nations of the world that have become overly dependent on oil for the life blood of their economies.[11]

While most versions of this prophecy see the *white serpent* as the Caucasians of America; the *red serpent* as either Russia, China, or both; and the *black serpent* as the black-robed Muslims, others see the *black serpent* as coming from Africa. Could this have reference to Boko Haran, an Islamic extremist group based in northeastern Nigeria, associated with the ISIS fighters of the Middle East and who are intent on killing all Christians and taking control of the entire world? Boko Haran announced its allegiance to the Islamic State of Iraq and the Levant and since its rise in 2009 has killed 20,000 people, displaced 2.3 million from their homes, and is listed as one of the world's deadliest terror groups.[12]

The Sign of the Son of Man

The *black serpent* would then stand on the *white serpent's* chest and boast of his victory. He would then look for another serpent to conquer.

First, he looked toward the *hilly country.* But the people looked so noble and erect that he decided to not fight them. Thus, he turned east, but was momentarily blinded by a great light brighter than the sun. The light was coming from the east over the waters. Once the *black serpent* regained his sight, he became terrified and headed south toward the sea and was never seen by the Indians again.[13]

> Note: The great light may well be the prophesied sign of the coming of the Savior, a sign that will be seen by all men together. The sign is said to be a brilliant light that comes out of the east. "*For as the light of the morning cometh out of the east, and shineth even unto the west, and covereth the whole earth, so shall also the coming of the Son of Man be.*" (Joseph Smith—Matthew 1:26)

Deganawida then noticed that a remnant of the *white serpent* (the Gentiles) had survived the attack. Although it was weak, it too saw the light and made a feeble attempt to move toward the light. The *white serpent* would eventually make its way to the *hilly country*, where the people there would help it.[14]

The Death of the Red Serpent

The form of the *red serpent* would rise again. He, too, had witnessed the strange light shining like a great star, and he had trembled with fear. As he tried to crawl toward the North Country, he would die from his many wounds along the way, leaving a bloody trail behind that would split this land of the Turtle in two, and then into four pieces. (America is referred to as Turtle Island by the Native Americans).[15]

Changes in the Weather

In the south, where the *black serpent* vanished, the ice would begin to melt and [hail] would fall, putting much of the land to the east into the deep sleep of winter.[16]

> 15 And there shall be weeping and wailing among the hosts of men;
>
> 16 And there shall be a great hailstorm sent forth to destroy the crops of the earth. (D&C 29:15–16)

Deganawida prophesied that the weather would become so unstable and the seas so violent that they would cover much of the country's old shoreline. New cliffs would rise out of the sea and new lands would appear. New mountains would form where the body of the *red serpent* lay, and a new sea would form in the North Country.[17]

In Doctrine and Covenants 61:14–16, we read the following:

> 14 Behold, I, the Lord, in the beginning blessed the waters; but in the last days, by the mouth of my servant John, I cursed the waters.
>
> 15 Wherefore, the days will come that no flesh shall be safe upon the waters.
>
> 16 And it shall be said in days to come that none is able to go up to the land of Zion upon the waters, but he that is upright in heart. (D&C 61:14–16)

Ushering In the Millennium

Deganawida prophesied that the mysterious light would eventually enshroud the entire earth in a mist like a giant cloud, and that *time* and *death* would cease to be. From the center of the mysterious light, the Great Star would begin to emerge. The light from this star is said to swell and eventually become even brighter than the Sun. Many things would be affected as people witness a *new world born before their eyes*.[18]

The City of Enoch Returns

Once the Star emerges, it is said that Deganawida would also emerge, and the people who had been hiding would come forth from their places of seclusion. They would be strange, as if they were walking for the first time. There would be many new colors and species of life that would come forth from the great void. During this time, man, beast, and all manner of life upon the earth would recognize and acknowledge their part in the spider web of life. All the creatures of the earth in that moment shall be as one, and man and beast shall communicate, and all fear shall flee away and be as nothing.

Deganawida prophesied that the people would witness the appearance of Deganawida, who would appear like he is walking right out of the Star (as a resurrected being?). It is said that he would be joined by many others and they would rejoice, for the people would once again walk in the way of the Great Peace. They would form a new and great civilization that would continue into forever. Then they would join with their brothers from the stars (resurrected beings?) and man and spirit shall be as one in the Great Peace. Finally, a great bow would appear in the heavens and it would ill sing the sounds of the new creation.[19]

The prophesied coming of Christ and the return of the city of Enoch has been an integral part of the gospel since the Restoration took place over a century and a half ago. Is it any wonder that it has also been an integral part of the spiritual teachings of the residue of Christ's New World flock (the Lamanite descendants of the ancient Nephite civilization) as well, however strange those teachings may seem? God has not forgotten Lehi's children of the forest, and great things await them in the winding-up scene of this earth, and the ushering in of the triumphant return of Christ.

Notes

1. "The Peacemaker's Prophecy," Mad Bear Anderson/Tuscarora, *Earth Mother Crying*, accessed March 20, 2017, earthmothercrying.org/iroquoisprophecy.htm.
2. "Red Elk's Version of Deganawidah," *Earth Mother Crying*, accessed March 20, 2017, earthmothercrying.org/iroquoisprophecy.htm.
3. Ezra Taft Benson, in Duane S. Crowther, *Prophecy: Key to the Future* (Bountiful, UT: Horizon Publishers, 1997), 12–13.
4. George Albert Smith, in David N. Balmforth, *America's Coming Crisis: Prophetic Warings, Divine Destiny* (Bountiful UT: Horizon Publishers, 1998), 123.
5. "Red Elk's Version of Deganawidah," *Earth Mother Crying.*
6. "The Peacemaker's Prophecy," Mad Bear Anderson/Tuscarora, *Earth Mother Crying.*
7. "Red Elk's Version of Deganawidah," *Earth Mother Crying.*
8. Ibid.
9. "The Peacemaker's Prophecy," Mad Bear Anderson/Tuscarora, *Earth Mother Crying.*
10. "Red Elk's Version of Deganawidah," *Earth Mother Crying.*
11. Sun Bear with Wabun Wind, *Black Dawn, Bright Day* (New York: Simon & Schuster, 1992), 41–42.
12. *Wikipedia*, s.v. "Boko Haran," last modified March 19, 2017, en.wikipedia.org/wiki/Boko_Haram.
13. "The Peacemaker's Prophecy," Mad Bear Anderson/Tuscarora, *Earth Mother Crying.*
14. "Red Elk's Version of Deganawidah," *Earth Mother Crying.*
15. Ibid.
16. Ibid.
17. Ibid.
18. Ibid.
19. Ibid.

13

Gathering to Utah

In the Prophet Deganawida's vison of the warring serpents, he saw many of the white serpents heading west to get as far away from the warfare going on in the east as they could. Under such circumstances, it is easy to expect that many Latter-day Saints living in such war-torn regions would also head west to likely join with the body of Saints living in the Rocky Mountains. Brigham Young spoke of a time in the future when a large number of Saints would gather to the West. He prophesied that the time would come when there would be a "great gulf between the righteous and the wicked" and that national intercourse between them would cease.[1] Regarding the Saints who made it to the Rockies in handcarts, he said,

> I am very thankful that so many of the brethren have come in with handcarts; my soul rejoiced. . . . Is this the end of it? No; there will be millions on millions that will come much in the same way, only they will not have handcarts, for they will take their bundles under their arms, and their children on their backs, and under their arms, and flee; and Zion's people will have to send out relief to them, for they will come when the judgments come on the nations.[2]

Noting such a time, Heber C. Kimball, first counselor to President Young, said, "Lay up your stores, and take your silks and fine things, and exchange them for grain and such things as you need, and the time will come when we will be obliged to depend upon our own resources; for the time is not far distant when the curtain will be dropped between us and the United States."[3]

In a *Deseret News* article in 1861, Brigham Young said,

> We are blessed in these mountains. This is the best place on earth for the Latter-day Saints. Search the history of all the nations and every geographical position on the face of the earth, and you cannot find another situation so well adapted for the Saints as are these mountains. Here is the place in which the Lord designed to hide his people. . . . It has been designed for many generations to hide up the Saints in the last days until the indignation of the Almighty be over.[4]

Gathering to the Stakes of Zion

In reference to Wilford Woodruff's warning voice about the future and the time when Utah would be a pretty good place to live, President Joseph Fielding Smith adds, "I believe Utah will be a pretty good place to live in, and other stakes of Zion, for I don't believe President Woodruff intended to confine this to the borders of Utah, but to the stakes of Zion. But the judgments of the Almighty are being poured out, and they shall continue, for the Prophet of God has said it. We shall not escape unless we repent, turn to the Lord, honor our Priesthood and our membership in this Church, and be true and faithful to our covenants."[5]

Any place the Church has been organized, you will find Zion. Brigham Young believed, "the time is nigh when every man that will not take up his sword against his neighbor must needs flee to Zion. Where is Zion? Where the organization of the Church of God is."[6] Thankfully, the Lord has given us prophets and apostles to warn and prepare us for such troubling times.

Harold B. Lee said,

> The spirit of gathering has been with the Church from the days of that restoration. Those who are of the blood of Israel, have a righteous desire after they are baptized, to gather together with the body of the Saints at the designated place. . . .
>
> After designating certain places in that day where the saints were to gather, the Lord said this:
>
> Until the day cometh when there is found no more room for them; and then I have other places which I will appoint unto them (D&C 101:21).[7]

In 1839, Joseph Smith made it clear that the various stakes of Zion, wherever they are, will be places of refuge for the Saints of the Most High. He said,

> There will be here and there a Stake [of Zion] for the gathering of the Saints. Some may have cried peace, but the Saints and the world will have little peace from henceforth. Let this not hinder us from going to the Stakes; for God has told us to flee, not dallying, or we shall be scattered, one here, and another there. . . .
>
> I prophesy, that . . . wars are at hand; we must not delay. . . . When wars come, we shall have to flee to Zion. The cry is to make haste.[8]

On another occasion, Joseph explained further:

> In addition to all temporal blessings, there is no other way for the Saints to be saved in these last days, [than by the gathering] as the concurrent testimony of all the holy Prophets clearly proves, for it is written—"They shall come from the east, and be gathered from the west; the north shall give up, and the south shall keep not back." "The sons of God shall be gathered from far, and His daughters from the ends of the earth."
>
> It is also concurrent testimony of all the Prophets, that this gathering together of all the Saints, must take place before the Lord comes to "take vengeance upon the ungodly," and "to be glorified and admitted by all those who obey the Gospel."[9]

Many of the Gentiles Will Join the Saints in the West

Orson Pratt noted that the time would come when the only body of people living the principles of a righteous government would be the Saints of God. Yet, he warns that if the Saints do not keep their covenants they too shall be inflicted. He said,

> If we will not keep the commandments of God, and if our rising generations will not give heed to the law of God and to the great light which has shone from Heaven in these latter days, but turn their hearts from the Lord their God and from the counsels of His priesthood, then we shall be visited like the wicked, then we shall have the hand of the Lord upon us in judgment; then that saying that the Lord has delivered in the Book of Doctrines and Covenants will be fulfilled upon us, "that I will visit Zion, if she does not do right, with sore afflictions, with pestilence, with sword, with famine and with the flame of devouring fire."[10]

Yet, Orson Pratt adds more:

> Let the righteous among this people abide in their righteousness, and let them cleave unto the Lord their God; and if there are those among them who will not keep his commandments, they will be cleansed out by the judgments of which I have spoken. But if the majority of this people will be faithful, the Lord will preserve them from their enemies, from sword, pestilence and plague and from every weapon that is lifted against them.[11]

It appears that the majority of the Saints will remain faithful, for several references have been made about the many souls that will join with the Saints during the tribulations, as despised as the Saints are now. Famine will also bring some Saints West. President Kimball said that the time would come when there would be millions of Gentiles that would be coming to us for want of bread, in much in the same way the early handcart people did.[12]

The Mountain West: A Refuge Forever

Although a large body of the Saints will ultimately help build up the New Jerusalem, some of the Saints living in the Rockies will remain behind in their mountain homes. Brigham Young said, "Remarks have been made as to our staying here [in the Rockies]. I will tell you how long we shall stay here. If we live our religion, we shall stay here in these mountains forever and forever, worlds without end, and a portion of the Priesthood will go and redeem and build up the centre Stake of Zion."[13]

President Brigham Young spoke of a vision he had (before the Saints were driven from Missouri in the early days of the Restoration) in which the members had been scattered in every direction. Yet, they returned to Jackson County from the west, which would certainly include the intermountain west.[14] Brigham Young said further,

> Are we going back to Jackson County? Yes. When? As soon as the way opens up. Are we all going? O no! of course not. The country is not large enough to hold our present numbers. When we do return there, will there be any less remaining in these mountains than we number today? No, there may be a hundred then for a single one that is there now. It is folly in men to suppose that we are going to break up these our hard earned homes to make others in a new country. We intend to hold our own here, and also penetrate the north and the south, the east and west, there to make others and to raise the ensign of truth.[15]

The Lord has always gathered the righteous out from among the wicked before the destruction comes. We learn of such gatherings in not just the Bible, but also in the Book of Mormon, where the Lord said to the wayward Nephites, "And the time speedily cometh, that except ye repent they [the Lamanites] shall possess the land of your inheritance, and the Lord God will lead away the righteous out from among you" (Jacob 3:4). The early Latter-day Saints were also surrounded by those who wanted to destroy them. Persecution escalated to the point where the Lord had to lead them away from their homes; He led them clear to the Rocky Mountains, where they were spared from most of the persecution and could grow and prosper as a people. Unfortunately, persecution is destined to rear its ugly head again in our day. And it will come at a time when the country itself is due for a cleansing. Thus, our trials will be multiplied.

The Cleansing of America

The cleansing of America with its accompanying wars, civil strife, invasions, and plagues appear to be at our very doorstep. When all hell breaks loose in America, the Lord will sweep the wicked of this country from off the face of the land, just as he did the Jaredites and the Nephites. Persecution of the Saints and rejection of the restored gospel of Jesus Christ seems to be a precursor to this terrible time of cleansing. The Lord said,

> And thus commandeth the Father that I should say unto you: At that day when the Gentiles shall sin against my gospel, and shall reject the fulness of my gospel, and shall be lifted up in the pride of their hearts above all nations, and above all the people of the whole earth, and shall be filled with all manner of lyings, and of deceits, and of mischiefs, and all manner of hypocrisy, and murders, and priestcrafts, and whoredoms, and of secret abominations; and if they shall do all those things, and shall reject the fulness of my gospel, behold, saith the Father, I will bring the fulness of my gospel from among them. (3 Nephi 16:10)

The Army of the Lord Is to Build Up the Center Stake of Zion

The Lord will need an army to redeem Zion—an army of righteous Saints who have learned through trials and tribulations to be the type of Saints that the Lord needs to build up the center stake of Zion. That army will not redeem the land through the shedding of blood, but it will be redeemed by power nonetheless. During the great heavenly manifestations that accompanied the dedication of the Kirtland Temple, one of Joseph Smith's scribes saw the "armies of heaven protecting the Saints in their return to Zion."[16]

What a glorious adventure and a day to remember that will be.

In Doctrine and Covenants 103, the Lord speaks of His presence going before those who are called to go back to Missouri to build up the New Jerusalem. Orson Pratt saw that scenario in the following way.

> We shall go back to Jackson County. Not that all this people will leave these mountains, or all be gathered together in a camp, but when we go back there will be a very large organization consisting of thousands, and tens of thousands, and they will march forward, the glory of God overshadowing their camp by day in the form of a cloud, and a pillar of flaming fire by night, the Lord's voice being uttered forth before his army. . . .
>
> Will not this produce terror upon all the nations of the earth? Will not armies of this description, though they may not be as numerous as the armies of the world, cause a terror to fall upon the nations? The Lord says the banners of Zion shall be terrible. If only one or two millions of this people were to go down and build the waste places of Zion, would it strike the people of Asia and Europe with terror? Not particularly, unless there was some supernatural power made manifest. But when the Lord's presence is there, when his voice is heard, and his angels go before the camp, it will be telegraphed to the uttermost parts of the earth and fear will seize upon all people, especially the wicked, and the knees of the ungodly will tremble in that day, and the high ones that are on high, and the great men of the earth.[17]

It is becoming increasingly difficult to ignore or dismiss the difficult days that have already descended upon our country. Yet the warning cry has been given, and the Saints have been called to gather to the stakes of Zion wherever they may be, at home or abroad, because the world is destined to be cleansed, not just America. Orson Pratt said the time will come when other governments will also tumble, and he described the arrival of others from foreign lands. He said,

> A flowing stream is one that runs continually; and the Gentiles will, in that day, come to us as a flowing stream, and we shall have to set our

> gates open continually, they will come as clouds and as doves in large flocks. Do you suppose that the Gentiles are going to be ignorant of what is taking place? "Now this will not be the case, they will perfectly understand what is taking place. The people will see that the hand of God is over this people; they will see that He is in our midst, and that He is our watchtower, that He is our shield and our defence, and therefore they will say, "Let us go up and put our riches in Zion, for there is no safety in our own nations."
>
> Those nations are trembling and tottering and will eventually crumble to ruin, and those men of wealth will come here, not to be baptized, but many of them will come that have never heard the servants of God; but they will hear that peace and health dwell among us, and that our officers are all peace officers, and our tax-gatherers men of righteousness.[18]

And what better place for them to come. It will only be among the Saints that the founding principles of our government are sustained and upheld.

> The day will come—and this is another prediction of Joseph Smith's—I want to remind you of it, my brethren and sisters, when good government, constitutional government—liberty—will be found among the Latter-day Saints, and it will be sought for in vain elsewhere; when the Constitution of this land and republican government and institutions will be upheld by this people who are now so oppressed and whose destruction is now sought so diligently. The day will come when the Constitution, and free government under it, will be sustained and preserved by this people.[19]

In his work *The Government of God*, John Taylor explained the Lord's position on the gathering of the righteous. He said,

> Before the Lord destroyed the old world, he directed Noah to prepare an ark; before the cities of Sodom and Gomorrah were destroyed, he told Lot to "flee to the mountains"; before Jerusalem was destroyed Jesus gave his disciples warning, and told them to "flee out of it;" and before the destruction of the world a message is sent; after this, the nations will be judged, for God is now preparing his own kingdom for his own reign, and will not be thwarted by any conflicting influence, or opposing power. *The testimony of God is first to be made known, the standard is to be raised, the Gospel of the kingdom is to be preached to all nations, the world is to be warned, and then come the troubles.* The whole

world is in confusion, morally, political, and religiously; but a voice was to be heard, "Come out of her, my people, that you partake not of her sins, and that ye receive not of her plagues."[20]

No Peace But in Zion and Her Stakes

Many of the stakes of Zion in the Rockies will be preserved on into the Millennium, for Joseph Smith prophesied, that "the Latter-day Saints who dwell in these mountains will stand in the flesh until the coming of the Son of Man. The Son of Man will come to them while in the Rocky Mountains."[21] Leading His flock to the Rocky Mountains after their expulsion from Missouri was divinely orchestrated. It provided a place of refuge when the storms begin to descend upon the nations. Yet, since that time, converts from all across the world have moved to the valleys of the Rockies. They have joined with the children of the covenant, and a mighty western empire of Latter-day Saints now exists, just as prophesied. Many more will yet join them as things heat up in the world. Yet, today, the Saints in foreign lands are encouraged to stay in their own homelands and build up stakes of Zion throughout the world. These stakes will be places of refuge for their people. Today, we are a world-wide church, and Zion is simply the place where the "pure in heart" (D&C 56:18) dwell. Thus, the great western empire in the Rockies will not be the only place of safety, neither will the New Jerusalem, but the stakes of Zion will provide safety wherever they are found.

The Entire Promised Land of America Is Zion

In 1844, Joseph Smith said,

> You know very well that the Lord has led this Church by revelation. I have another revelation in relation to economy of this Church—a great, grand, and glorious revelation. . . .You know there has been a great discussion in relation to Zion—where it is, and where the gathering of the dispensation is, and which I am now going to tell you. The prophets have spoken and written upon it; but I will make a proclamation that will cover a broader ground. *The whole of America is the Zion itself, from north to south, and is described by the Prophets, who declared that it is Zion where the mountain of the Lord should be, and that it should be in the center of the land. . . .*
>
> *I have received instructions from the Lord that from henceforth wherever the Elders of Israel shall build up churches and branches unto*

> *the Lord throughout the States, there shall be a stake of Zion. In the great cities, as Boston, New York, &c., there shall be stakes.* It is a glorious proclamation.[22]

This proclamation appears to deal exclusively with the United States of America not both North and South America as some have supposed), because "states," not countries, were noted in this proclamation. Yet, since that proclamation, the Church has spread into nearly every land and country on earth, with the stakes and churches built up in each land as places designated for the gathering of the Saints. Because of the concern that so many have about the coming storm and the gathering of the Saints, President Harold B. Lee spoke several times about the fallacious notion that only those in the Rocky Mountains will find safety. He said,

> Clearly, the Lord has placed the responsibility for directing the work of gathering in the hands of the leaders of the Church to whom he will reveal his will where and when such gathering would take place in the future. It would be well before the frightening events concerning the fulfillment of all God's promises and predictions are upon us, that the Saints in every land prepare themselves and look forward to the instructions that shall come to them from the First Presidency of this Church as to where they shall be gathered and not be disturbed in their feelings until such instruction is given to them as it is revealed by the Lord to the proper authority.[23]

World events leave us feeling uneasy about the future of our country, and even the world. We wonder just how close we are to the winding up scene of the earth, prophesied by so many of the prophets of God. We worry particularly about those prophecies in the book of Revelation that speak of world conflicts, famines, and the coming of Armageddon. It would be hard not to be concerned with the bad news that is paraded before our eyes every waking minute of the day via television and social media. Yet, we must take comfort in the knowledge that God is in control, and He will do nothing without first informing His duly appointed servants who have been planning and preparing for such events for a long time now. He will make it known to the Saints when the time comes. Thus, we need not unnecessarily fear or plan our own escape, but wait patiently upon the good time of the Lord for any changes that need to be made in our current circumstances—changes that will come by way of the Lord's dully appointed servants to those of their individual flocks.

Notes

1. Brigham Young, in *Journal of Discourses*, 12:284.
2. Young, in *Journal of Discourses*, 4:106.
3. Heber C. Kimball, in *Journal of Discourses*, 5:10.
4. Young, in *Journal of Discourses*, 9:3, 2.
5. Joseph Fielding Smith, in *Conference Report*, April 1937, 62.
6. Young, in *Journal of Discourses*, 8:205.
7. Harold B. Lee, "The Spirit of Gathering," *Improvement Era*, May 1948, 320.
8. Joseph Smith, in *History of the Church*, 3:390.
9. Ibid., 4:272.
10. Orson Pratt, in *Journal of Discourses*, 12:345.
11. Ibid., 15:362.
12. Kimball, in *Journal of Discourses*, 4:109–10.
13. Young, in *Journal of Discourses*, 11:16.
14. Ibid., 11:17.
15. Ibid., 18:355–56.
16. *History of the Church*, 2:381.
17. Pratt, in *Journal of Discourses*, 15:364.
18. Ibid., 3:16.
19. George Q. Cannon, in *Journal of Discourses*, 23:104.
20. Gerald N. Lund, *The Coming of the Lord* (Salt Lake City: Bookcraft, 2002), 85; italics in original.
21. Wilford Woodruff, in *Conference Report*, April 1898, 102.
22. Joseph Smith, in *History of the Church*, 6:318–19; italics in original.
23. Lund, *The Coming of Christ*, 94–95.

14

The Gathering to the New Jerusalem

Throughout all the ages of history, the Lord has always warned and forewarned His people of impending perils and when to flee if necessary. In a comforting message to the Saints, may we repeat President John Taylor's reminder of God's care and concern for the faithful:

> *The testimony of God is first to be made known, the standard is to be raised, the Gospel of the kingdom is to be preached to all nations, the world is to be warned, and then comes the troubles.* The whole world is in confusion; morally, politically, and religiously; but a voice was to be heard, "Come out of her, my people, that you partake not of her sins, and that ye receive not of her plagues."[1]

The Lord's warning voice includes inviting us to share the gospel, so that the lost sheep of the His flock might be gathered in from the four corners of the earth to Zion. Joseph Smith spoke on that subject and on related revelations from the Lord. He reported,

> 5 Verily I say unto you all: Arise and shine forth, that thy light may be a standard for the nations:
>
> 6 And that the gathering together upon the land of Zion, and upon her stakes, may be for a defense, and for a refuge from the storm, and from wrath when it shall be poured out without mixture upon the whole earth. (D&C 115:5–6)

Joseph Smith also taught the following in relation to the gathering of Israel,

> Much has been said and done of late by the general government in relation to the Indians (Lamanites) within the territorial limits of the United States. One of the most important points in the faith of the Church of the Latter-day Saints, through the fullness of the everlasting Gospel, is the gathering of Israel (of whom the Lamanites constitute a part) that happy time when Jacob shall go up to the house of the Lord, to worship Him in spirit and in truth, to live in holiness; when the Lord will restore His judges as at the first, and His counselors as at the beginning. . . .
>
> In speaking of the gathering, we mean to be understood as speaking of it according to scripture, the gathering of the elect of the Lord out of every nation on earth, and bringing them to the place of the Lord of Hosts, when the city of righteousness shall be built, and where the people shall be of one heart and one mind, when the Savior comes; yea, where the people shall walk with God like Enoch, and be free from sin. The word of the Lord is precious; and when we read that the veil spread over all nations will be destroyed, and the pure in heart see God, and reign with Him a thousand years on earth, we want all honest men to have a chance to gather and build up a city of righteousness, where even upon the bells of the horses shall be written "*Holiness to the Lord.*"[2]

In speaking of Zion, the Lord revealed to Joseph Smith:

> 21 Therefore, verily, thus saith the Lord, let Zion rejoice, for this is Zion—the pure in heart; therefore, let Zion rejoice, while all the wicked shall mourn.
>
> 22 For behold, and lo, vengeance cometh speedily upon the ungodly as the whirlwind; and who shall escape it?
>
> 23 The Lord's scourge shall pass over by night and by day, and the report thereof shall vex all people; yea, it shall not be stayed until the Lord come;
>
> 24 For the indignation of the Lord is kindled against their abominations and all their wicked works.
>
> 25 Nevertheless, Zion shall escape if she observe to do all things whatsoever I have commanded her.
>
> 26 But if she observe not to do whatsoever I have commanded her, I will visit her according to all her works, with sore affliction, with pestilence, with plague, with sword, with vengeance, with devouring fire. (D&C 97:21–26)

A Warning from the Lord

The time is shortly coming when bloodshed will wipe the wicked away in order to prepare the way for the lost tribes of Israel to be gathered with the just into the New Jerusalem. Joseph Smith said,

> And now I am prepared to say by the authority of Jesus Christ, that not many years shall pass away before the United States shall present such a scene of *bloodshed* as has not a parallel in the history of our nation; pestilence, hail, famine, and earthquake will sweep the wicked of this generation from off the face of the land, to open and prepare the way for the return of the lost tribes of Israel from the north country. . . . Therefore I declare unto you the warning which the Lord has commanded me to declare unto this generation, remembering that the eyes of my Maker are upon me, and that to Him I am accountable for every word I say, wishing nothing worse to my fellow-men than their eternal salvation; therefore, "Fear God, and give glory to Him, for the hour of His judgment is come." Repent ye, repent ye, and embrace the everlasting covenant, and flee to Zion, before the overflowing scourge overtake you.[3]

Gathering to the Center Stake of Zion

The Lord has designed Jackson County, Missouri, as the center stake of Zion. The glorious city yet to be built will be called the New Jerusalem. He said,

> 66 And it shall be called the New Jerusalem, a land of peace, a city of refuge, a place of safety for the saints of the Most High God;
>
> 67 And the glory of the Lord shall be there, and the terror of the Lord also shall be there, insomuch that the wicked will not come unto it, and it shall be called Zion. (D&C 45:66–67)

The Assembling of the Saints to Zion

Joseph Smith taught,

> The building up of Zion is a cause that has interested the people of God in every age; it is a theme upon which prophets, priests and kings have dwelt with peculiar delight; they have looked forward with joyful anticipation to the day in which we live; and fired with heavenly and joyful anticipations they have sung and written and prophesied of this our day; but they died without the sight; we are the favored people that God had made choice of to bring about the Latter-day glory; it is left

> for us to see, participate in and help to roll forward the Latter-day glory, "the dispensation of the fullness of times, when God will gather together all things that are in heaven, and all things that are upon the earth, "even in one," when the Saints of God will be gathered in one from every nation,and kindred, and people, and tongue, when the Jews will be gathered together into one, the wicked will also be gathered together to be destroyed, as spoken of by the prophets; the Spirit of God will also dwell with His people, and be withdrawn from the rest of the nations, and all things whether in heaven or on earth will be in one, even in Christ. The heavenly Priesthood will unite with the earthly, to bring about those great purposes; and whilst we are thus united in one common cause, to roll forth the kingdom of God, the heavenly Priesthood are not idle spectators, the Spirit of God will be showered down from above, and it will dwell in our midst. The blessings of the Most High will rest upon our tabernacles, and our name will be handed down to future ages; our children will rise up and call us blessed; and generations yet unborn will dwell with peculiar delight upon the scenes that we have passed through, the privations that we have endured; the untiring zeal that we have manifested; the all but insurmountable difficulties that we have overcome in laying the foundation of a work that brought about the glory and blessing which they will realize; a work that God and angels have contemplated with delight for generations past; that fired the souls of the ancient patriarchs and prophets; a work that is destined to bring about the destruction of the powers of darkness, the renovation of the earth, the glory of God, and the salvation of the human family.[4]

Joseph Fielding Smith describes how he sees the great exodus of the Saints to Jackson County, Missouri. He said the following:

> When God leads the people back to Jackson County, how will he do it? Let me picture to you how some of us may be gathered and led to Jackson County. I think I see two or three hundred thousand people wending their way across the great plain enduring the nameless hardships of the journey, herding and guarding their cattle by day and by night, and defending themselves and little ones from foes on the right hand and on the left, as when they came here. They will find the journey back to Jackson County will be as real as when they came out here. Now, mark it. And though you may be led by the power of God "with a stretched out arm," it will not be more manifest than the leading the people out here to those that participate in it. They will think there are a great many hardships to endure in this manifestation of the power of God, and it will be left, perhaps to their children to see the gory of their deliverance,

> just as it is left for us to see the glory of our former deliverance from the hands of those that sought to destroy us. Thus is one way to look at it. It is certainly a practical view. Some might ask, what will become of the railroads? I fear that the sifting process would be insufficient were we to travel by railroads. We are apt to overlook the manifestations of the power of God to us because we are participators in them, and regard them as commonplace events. But when it is written in history—as it will be written—it will be shown forth to future generations as one of the most marvelous, unexampled and unprecedented accomplishments that has even been known to history.[5]

Although the Saints have been promised protection from the major calamities of the last days as the end time approaches, we cannot say that there will not be pain or death for the righteous who succumb to the weakness of the flesh or to the woes brought about by those whose mission it is to destroy and lay waste. Yet those who fall will have a glorious reward—equal to that of all the other martyrs who have given their lives in the cause of righteous—and will help to assure the wicked receive their just rewards. But the Saints as a whole will prevail over their enemies and, when the time is right, will be gathered out from those areas destined for destruction and given sanctuary within the stakes of Zion (see D&C 103:5–7).

A Remnant of Jacob Shall Also Help Build the New Jerusalem

Although remnants of Jacob's house of Israel were scattered worldwide, Joseph Smith maintained that the remnants of Jacob's favorite son, Joseph, will also be part of the rise of New Jerusalem. The Lord and His servants have much to say about the Lamanites. In the *Millennial Star*, we read from the "The Proclamation of the Twelve Apostles of the Church of Jesus Christ of Latter-Day Saints," "Greeting: Know ye: That the kingdom of God has come: as has been predicted by ancient prophets, and prayed for in all ages; even that kingdom which shall fill the whole earth, and shall stand forever."[6] Then, after a long list of declarations about the advent of the Restoration and all that it entails (including some of the sobering events of the last days), the Twelve mention the blessings waiting the natives of America:. They continue:

While these great events are rolling on the wheels of time, and being fulfilled in the old world, the Western Continent will present a scene of grandeur, greatness, and glory, far surpassing the scene just described.

The Lord will make her that halted a remnant; and gather her that was driven out and afflicted; and make her who was cast afar off, a strong nation; and will reign over *them* in Mount Zion from that time forth and for ever.

Or, in other words, He will assemble the Natives the remnants of Joseph in America; and make of them a great, and strong, and powerful nation: and he will civilize and enlighten them and will establish a holy city, and temple, and seat of government among them, which shall be called Zion.

And there shall be his tabernacle, his sanctuary, his throne, and seat of government for the whole continent of North and South America for ever.

In short, it will be to the western hemisphere what Jerusalem will be to the eastern.

And there the Messiah will visit them in person; and the old Saints, who will then have been raised from the dead, will be with him. And he will establish his kingdom and laws over all the land. . . .

The despised and degraded son of the forest, who has wandered in dejection and sorrow, and suffered reproach, shall then drop his disguise, and stand forth in manly dignity, and exclaim to the Gentiles who have envied and sold him: "*I am Joseph: does my father yet live?*" Or, in other words: I am a descendant of that Joseph who was sold into Egypt. You have hated *me*, and sold *me*, and thought *I* was dead. But lo! I live, and am heir to the inheritance, titles, honors, priesthood, sceptre, crown, throne, and eternal life and dignity of my fathers who live for evermore.

He shall then be ordained, washed, anointed with holy oil and arrayed in fine linen, even in the glorious and beautiful garments and royal robes of the high priesthood, which is after the order of the Son of God; and shall enter into the congregation of the Lord, even into the Holy of Holies, there to be crowned with authority and power which shall never end. . . .

He shall also behold his Redeemer and be filled with his presence, while the cloud of his glory shall be seen in his temple.[7]

The Native Americans to Become a Righteous Branch

The remnant seed of Lehi, or the Lamanites, have much yet to do in the fulfilling of prophecies relative to America—the land the Lord gave them as an eternal inheritance, but only after they returned to the fold and joined with the Saints of the Most High. Eventually, the Lamanites will become a righteous branch of Israel and will be a comely people. The Lord will be with them, and they will be numbered among the house of Joseph. The destined premillennial refinement and blossoming of the Lamanites is spoken of by the Lord:

> 23 Wherefore, be not deceived, but continue in steadfastness, looking forth for the heavens to be shaken, and the earth to tremble and to reel to and fro as a drunken man, and for the valleys to be exalted, and for the mountains to be made low, and for the rough places to become smooth—and all this when the angel shall sound his trumpet.
>
> 24 But before the great day of the Lord shall come, Jacob shall flourish in the wilderness, and the Lamanites shall blossom as the rose. (D&C 49:23–24)

Spencer W. Kimball reminded us to treat the Lamanites as brothers and sisters, for even our own ancestors were wayward at times,

> Truly our paths have met once more—we, a mixed remnant of Israel, principally Ephraim, even referred to as Gentiles, now come forth out of captivity (see, e.g., 1 Nephi 13:19, 39, a people with a long history of apostasy and darkness and persecution, now only through the grace of Almighty God restored to the blessings of the gospel, that we in turn might be a blessing to the nations of the earth; and the Lamanites, also a people of disobedience now returned to the fold, whose suffering have been sore, and punishment severe, and humiliation complete, whose affliction these many centuries must certainly be fruit meet for repentance. And what should be the nature of our reunion? We are relatives. We are brothers and sisters under the skin. We should receive each other with great joy.[8]

The Lamanites to Help Build the New Jerusalem

In their more refined state, the Lamanites will also be privileged to take part in the construction of the New Jerusalem, according the prophecies of Ether:

> 4 Behold, Ether saw the days of Christ, and he spake concerning a New Jerusalem upon this land.

> 5 And he spake also concerning the house of Israel, and the Jerusalem from whence Lehi should come—after it should be destroyed it should be built up again, a holy city unto the Lord; wherefore, it could not be a new Jerusalem for it had been in a time of old; but it should be built up again, and become a holy city of the Lord; and it should be built unto the house of Israel—
>
> 6 And that a New Jerusalem should be built up upon this land, unto the remnant of the seed of Joseph, for which things there has been a type. . . .
>
> 8 Wherefore, the remnant of the house of Joseph shall be built upon this land; and it shall be a land of their inheritance; and they shall build up a holy city unto the Lord, like unto the Jerusalem of old; and they shall no more be confounded, until the end come when the earth shall pass away. . . .
>
> 10 And they are they who are numbered among the remnant of the seed of Joseph, who were of the house of Israel. (Ether 13:4–6, 8, 10)

When tribe after tribe passes through the gates of Zion, the hills will sing their everlasting praises to God, and the lost sons of Israel will mingle with the gathered of Ephraim, and together they will await the triumphant return of Jehovah.

The City of Zion

Joseph Smith was shown in vision, the dimensions of the city of Zion. In general conference, Wilford Woodruff gave us this information. He said, "Joseph presented us in some degree the plot of the city of Kirtland (which is the stronghold of the daughter of Zion)."[9] The plan that he presented was given to him by vision, and the future will prove that the vision of Joseph, concerning Jackson County, Missouri, and all the various stakes of Zion and the redemption of Israel will be fulfilled in the time appointed of the Lord.

Orson Pratt said:

> We shall in due time walk forth into Jackson County and build up the waste places of Zion. We shall build a beautiful city after the order and pattern that the Lord shall reveal, . . . God intends to have a city built up that will never be destroyed nor overcome, but that will exist while eternity shall endure; and he will point out the pattern and show the order of architecture; he will show unto his servants the nature of the streets and the pavement thereof, the kind of precious stones that shall

> enter into the buildings, the nature of the rock and precious stones that will adorn the gates and the walls of that city; for the gates will be open continually says the prophet Isaiah that men may bring in the forces of the Gentiles.[10]

These heavenly designed cities will be without congestion and crime and the moral decay our poor cities endure today. With heavenly guidance, men will work for the common good of all men, which will bring them the greatest blessing of education, culture, and spiritual growth. Men and women alike will be trained to draw upon revelation for further light and knowledge, and both resurrected beings and angels will descend to teach and tutor them in the things of God. Love will be the grand key and the great force that will unite humanity during a thousand years of millennial peace.

The City of Zion, the Pure in Heart

The keys for directing this temple-oriented society were given to Joseph Smith in the Kirtland Temple in 1836. The Lord made known to him at that time that these manifestations were just the beginning of the blessings that were destined to fall upon His people (see D&C 110:10). Joseph Smith said,

> Truly this is a day long to be remembered by the Saints of the last days,—a day in which the God of heaven has begun to restore the ancient order of His kingdom unto His servants and His people—a day in which all things are concurring to bring about the completion of the fullness of the Gospel, a fullness of the dispensation of dispensations, even the fullness of times; a day in which God has begun to make manifest and set in order in His Church those things which have been, and those things which the ancient prophets and wise men desired to see but died without beholding them; a day in which those things begin to be made manifest, which have been hid from before the foundation of the world, and which Jehovah has promised should be made known in His own due time unto His servants, to prepare the earth for the return of His glory even a celestial glory, and a kingdom of Priests and kings to God and the Lamb, forever, on Mount Zion, and with him the hundred and forty and four thousand whom John the Revelator saw, all of which is to come to pass in the restitution of all things.[11]

No more will the wicked rule their religions by the sword, or slaughter millions who oppose this god or that. The crusades of past ages, and even the battles in these latter-days, will no longer come to mind or be remembered; in God's society, the needs of the people both spiritually and temporally will be met by a king who will serve His people with perfect love—that being Jesus Christ. He will measure out justice in total and complete righteous. Prophets have proclaimed from the earliest of times that Christ would one day sit upon His throne and rule the world. The angel Gabriel carried that message to the young virgin Mary when he told her that she would conceive and bear the Son of God:

> 32 He shall be great, and shall be called the Son of the Highest; and the Lord God shall give unto him the throne of his father David:
>
> 33 And he shall reign over the house of Jacob for ever: and of his kingdom there shall be no end. (Luke 1:32–33)

During the millennial reign of the savior, men will no longer live in fear of false judges or corrupt societies because the Son of God will rule His kingdom in perfect righteous. The law will go forth from Zion to all the nations of the world, and will teach men everywhere how to live in peace.

Brigham Young taught,

> When the world is in a state of true civilization, man will have ceased to contend against his fellow-man, either as individuals, parties, communities, sects, or nations This state of civilization will be brought about by the holy Priesthood of the Son of God; and men, with full purpose of heart will seek unto him who is pure and holy, even our Great Creator—our Father and God; and he will give them a law that is pure—a government and plan of society possessed by holy beings in heaven. Then there will be no more war, no more bloodshed, no more evil speaking and evil doing; but all will be contented to follow in the path of truth, which alone is calculated to exalt and dignify the whole man, mentally and physically, in all his operations, labours, and purposes. Short of this, mankind cannot be said to be truly civilized.[12]

In man's idea of Utopia, men and woman are portrayed as childlike in nature. They neither sweat nor toil. They laugh and play in a state of perpetual innocence and thus remain in their state of innocence forever. How can a fulness of joy be found in such a society? Where is the growth of human potential and intellect? God has placed a treasury of knowledge at our feet, and only by grasping for it can we learn the mysteries of the universe and reach our full potential and the state of happiness man has been searching for since the world began. With Satan bound for those thousand years, man can progress upward and onward toward perfection.

The struggles associated with living in this pre-apocalyptic age and the rise of the New Jerusalem are but a prologue to the cleansing that will take place just prior to the Savior's Second Coming. Just as it was in the meridian of time when the Savior visited the Nephites after His death and Resurrection, the more wicked part of the people of the world must be cleansed before the Savior comes. Thus, hard times lie ahead, but glory awaits the righteous who endure.

Notes

1. Gerald N. Lund, *The Coming of the Lord* (Salt Lake City: Bookcraft, 2002), 85; italics in original.
2. Joseph Fielding Smith, arr., *Teachings of the Prophet Joseph Smith*, 3rd ed. (Salt Lake City: Deseret News Press, 1942), 92–93.
3. Ibid., 17–18.
4. Joseph Smith, *History of the Church*, 3:609–10.
5. Joseph Fielding Smith, in *Journal of Discourses*, 24:156–57.
6. "Proclamation of the Twelve Apostles of The Church of Jesus Christ of Latter-day Saints," *Millennial Star*, April 6, 1845; italics in original.
7. Ibid.
8. Spencer W. Kimball, *Teachings of Spencer W. Kimball* (Salt Lake City: The Church of Jesus Christ of Latter-day Saints, 2012), 596. See also, Daniel C. Peterson, *The Last Day: Teachings of the Modern Prophets* (Aspen Books, 1998), 1:227.
9. Journal of Wilford Woodruff, April 6, 1837.
10. Orson Pratt, *Journal of Discourses*, 15:365.
11. Joseph Smith, *History of the Church*, 3:492–93.
12. Brigham Young, in *Journal of Discourses*, 8:7.

15

The Ushering In of the Millennium

Note: Excerpts taken from author's previous book, *The Millennium: A Journey Through the Sabbath of Time.*[1]

Mighty changes are destined to take place on the earth at the time of the Savior's coming. "Every valley shall be exalted, and every mountain and hill shall be made low . . . and the rough places plain" (Isaiah 40:4).

"For, behold, I create new heavens and a new earth: and the former shall not be remembered, nor come into mind" (Isaiah 65:17).

Once the corruptible things of the earth are forgotten, the earth will once again be a paradise. Deserts will be gardens; rivers, streams, and fresh pools of water will replace parched ground; and the earth will finally be able to rest from her labors and enjoy a Sabbath of peace. It is hard to imagine the earth being more beautiful than it is today (except for the carnage that man has inflicted upon her). Joseph Smith describes his view of the area around Jackson Country in his day:

> As far as the eye can reach the beautiful rolling prairies lie spread out like a sea of meadows; and are decorated with a growth of flowers so gorgeous and grand as to exceed description; and nothing is more fruitful, or a richer stockholder in the blooming prairie than the honey bee. Only on the water courses is timber to be found. There in strips from one to three miles in width, and following faithfully the meanderings of the streams, it grows in luxuriant forests. The forests are a mixture of oak, hickory, black walnut, elm, ash, cherry, honey

> locust, mulberry, coffee bean, hackberry, boxelder, and bass wood; with the addition of cottonwood, butterwood, pecan, and soft and hard maple upon the bottoms. The shrubbery is beautiful, and consists in part of plums, grapes, crab apple, and persimmons.
>
> The soil is rich and fertile; from three to ten feet deep, and generally composed of a rich black mold, intermingled with clay and sand. It yields in abundance. . . . Buffalo, elk, deer, bear, wolves, beaver and many smaller animals here roam at pleasure. Turkeys, geese, swans, ducks, and a variety of the feathered tribe, are among the rich abundance that grace the delightful regions of this goodly land.[2]

If these beautiful temporal scenes delight our senses and give us joy, we can only imagine what beauty awaits us in the earth's terrestrial state when the earth becomes a "global" Garden of Eden, filled with flora and fauna of every description. We can imagine flowers that bloom spontaneously, flowers of magnificent beauty and colors of every hue, and meadows ablaze with dazzling blossoms that seem to dance in the afternoon breeze. We can visualize broad grasslands, sweeping prairies, and an infinite variety of trees gracing emerald green forests, each providing fruit and nutmeats for the taking. Freshwater lakes, ponds, streams, and waterfalls will dot the landscape, and the cry of the loon and other waterfowl will be heard across the land. Songbirds will also sing their melodies and even the soft murmurings of insects will please the ear. Yet, without a doubt, anything our finite minds can imagine will pale in comparison to the glorious scenes that will await us.

In Isaiah, we read, "For the Lord shall comfort Zion: he will comfort all her waste places; and he will make her wilderness like Eden, and her desert like the garden of the LORD; joy and gladness shall be found therein, thanksgiving, and the voice of melody" (Isaiah 51:3).

Other great blessings await us as well. As the earth transitions from its current telestial state to a more glorious terrestrial order, man and beast will interact peacefully for the first time since Adam and Eve walked the Garden of Eden.

Animals of every kind and description will roam the land in peace, and vegetation will sustain them. All animosity between man and beast will at long last and forever be done away with during the great day of the Lord.

6 The wolf also shall dwell with the lamb, and the leopard shall lie down with the kid; and the calf and the young lion and the fatling together; and a little child shall lead them.

7 And the cow and the bear shall feed; their young ones shall lie down together; and the lion shall eat straw like the ox.

8 And the suckling child shall play on the hole of the asp, and the weaned child shall put is hand on the cockatrice' den.

9 They shall not hurt nor destroy in all my holy mountain; for the earth shall be full of the knowledge of the Lord, as the waters cover the sea (Isaiah11:6–9).

What a wonderful time to live in. To be able to mingle with various beasts and enjoy their companionship is an exciting concept. Their gentle natures, their intelligence, and beauty will be magnified, and man will be able to interact with them peacefully and without fear of any kind.

24 For all old things shall pass away, and all things shall become new, even the heaven and the earth . . . both men and beasts, the fowls of the air, and the fishes of the sea;

25 And not one hair, neither mote, shall be lost, for it is the workmanship of mine hand. (D&C 29:24–25)

Man, too, will enjoy a new state of contentment. His anger, pride, and carnal nature will be replaced with his more noble characteristics, and in his renewed state he will love God and righteousness. To add to this happy state, that old serpent, the devil, will at long last be bound and will cease to be a plague to mankind.

In 1 Nephi, we read, "And because of the righteousness of his people, Satan has no power; wherefore, he cannot be loosed for the space of many years; for he hath no power over the hearts of the people, for they dwell in righteousness, and the Holy One of Israel reigneth" (1 Nephi 22:26).

The Great Change

Perhaps one of the greatest changes to take place during the Millennium will be the change from our mortal condition to that of a resurrected being in the twinkling of an eye.

29 And there shall be no sorrow because there is no death.

> 30 In that day an infant shall not die until he is old; and his life shall be as the age of a tree;
>
> 31 And when he dies he shall not sleep, that is to say in the earth, but shall be changed in the twinkling of an eye, and shall be caught up, and his rest shall be glorious. (D&C 101:29–31)

Man's capacity to learn will also be heightened during the Millennium, and he will delight in searching out those mysteries that have plagued mankind since the beginning of time. By the power of the Holy Ghost, knowledge will increase until man will be privileged to understand things that the angels in heaven have been holding in reserve until the fulness of time, such as whether there be one God or many, and other such mysteries.

> 29 All thrones and dominions, principalities and powers, shall be revealed and set forth upon all who have endured valiantly for the gospel of Jesus Christ.
>
> 30 And also, if there be bounds set to the heavens or to the seas, or to the dry land, or to the sun, moon, or stars—
>
> 31 All the times of their revolutions; all the appointed days, months, and years, and all the days of their days, months, and years, and all their glories, laws, and set times, shall be revealed in the days of the dispensation of the fulness of times. (D&C 121:29–31)

We will be taught by heavenly beings, and Jesus Christ himself, who will preach sermons never heard before. Our hearts will leap with joy at the marvelous revelations that will come forth at that time:

> 32 Yea, verily I say unto you, in that day when the Lord shall come, he shall reveal all things—
>
> 33 Things which have passed, and hidden things which no man knew, things of the earth, by which it was made, and the purpose and the end thereof—
>
> 34 Things most precious, things that are above, and things that are beneath, things that are in the earth, and upon the earth, and in heaven. (D&C 101:32–34)

Christ will impart all wisdom and knowledge to those who thirst. If a man asks, it will be given him and nothing shall be withheld. "For since the beginning of the world men have not heard, nor perceived by the ear, neither hath the eye seen, O God, beside thee, what he hath prepared for him that waiteth for him." (Isaiah 64:4)

The Day of the Lord, or the Sabbath of time, occurs six thousand years after the creation of mankind, and the Sabbath of time continues on for another thousand years of peace and harmony. Those thousand years will be a time when man will produce more good works, enlightened thoughts, beautiful edifices, grand cities, magnificent artworks, and splendid music than we ever dreamed possible. Nothing our minds can imagine will compare with the beauty and glory that awaits the faithful during the great day of the Lord.

As the divine Spirit rains down upon the land and its inhabitants, knowledge will begin to flood the earth, including those mysteries that were hidden from the foundation of the world. Things both past, present, and future will be made known to the millennial man and woman and there will be nothing that will be withheld from their eyes. The knowledge of the world and of the entire universe will be laid out before them in all their splendor.

> 15 The earth shall be full of the knowledge of the Lord as the waters cover the sea.
>
> 16 Wherefore, the things of all nations shall be made known; yea, all things shall be made known unto the children of men.
>
> 17 There is nothing which is secret save it shall be revealed; there is no work of darkness save it shall be made manifest in the light; and there is nothing which is sealed upon the earth save it shall be loosed.
>
> 18 Therefore, all things which have been revealed unto the children of men shall at that day be revealed. (2 Nephi 30:15–18)

The City of Zion

Although Zion will ultimately fill up the whole earth, its noble beginnings will be in Jackson County, Missouri, at a time when the world is filled with warring and contention. This glorious city will continue to stand through the destruction of the last days and will become a beacon to the righteous who will seek refuge at her gates. Prophets from all dispensations have prophesied about that glorious time and have longed to be a part of that great millennial society. John Taylor elaborated on the glory of the Zion to come:

> We believe that we shall rear splendid edifices, magnificent temples and beautiful cities that shall become the pride, praise and glory of the whole earth. We believe that this people will excel in literature, in science and the arts and in manufactures. In fact, there will be a concentration of wisdom, not only of the combined wisdom of the world as it now exists, but men will be inspired in regard to all these matters in a manner and to an extent that they never have been before, and we shall have eventually, when the Lord's purposes are carried out, the most magnificent buildings . . . [the] most costly clothing, and be the most healthy and the most intellectual people that will reside upon the earth. This is part and parcel of our faith. . . . This is only a faint outline of some of our views in relation to these things, and hence we talk of returning to Jackson County to build the most magnificent temple that ever was formed on the earth and the most splendid city that was ever erected; yea, cities, if you please. The architectural designs of those splendid edifices, cities, walls, gardens, bowers, streets, &c., will be under the direction of the Lord, who will control and manage all these matters; and the people, from the President down, will all be under the guidance and direction of the Lord in all the pursuits of human life, until eventually they will be enabled to erect cities that will be fit to be caught up—that when Zion descends from above, Zion will also ascend from beneath, and be prepared to associate with those from above. The people will be so perfected and purified, ennobled, exalted, and dignified in their feelings and so truly humble and most worthy, virtuous and intelligent that they will be fit, when caught up, to associate with that Zion that shall come down from God out of heaven. This is the idea, in brief, that we have entertained in relation to many of these things.[3]

The Millennium will not be a time of leisure or idleness, for there will be much work to do. There will be farming and merchandising. Homes and cities must be built, temples erected and temple work attended to. Fortunately, man will not weary of his work and responsibilities since the quickened man will no longer know the aches and pains of mortality, or succumb to illness or disease. He will not be crippled or become depressed or mentally anguished, nor will he will suffer the debilitating effects of old age. What wonderful things we could accomplish in this life if the handicaps of the flesh did not fetter us or keep us down. Nonetheless, this life is a time and place for learning and for being tested and tried. All of our experiences, whether good or bad, are for our ultimate benefit.

Those so blessed to be born during the Millennium will not have to pass through the portals of pain and despair, but regardless, they too must work out their salvation. They must grow step-by-step—gaining knowledge precept upon precept just as mortal man did—and must use their agency to do good works and labor for their support and for that of their families. They must search for and find mates, marry within the holy temples, and raise up righteous children to the Lord. They must worship and pray and search the scriptures for the meaning of life. They must learn to draw upon the powers of heaven and seek revelation from on high. They must help in the work of salvation for their kindred dead and must help in the work of reconciliation for the entire human family, for all things must be in order. Families must be sealed, partners married, and ordinances recorded in such a way that they coincide with the records of heaven. A great work must be done—a work that will take a millennium to complete and the millennial family must be the means of its completion.

Those who live during the Sabbath of time will not be idle or pampered or living lives of perpetual luxury, but they will be united in love and purpose. They will work together to complete the work of sealing the entire human family together so that the Son can present the finished work to His Father when the allotted time is finished. There will be more work to do during the Millennium than in all past dispensations combined. It will be a time of temple work, genealogy work, and of the reconciling of all things.

With the earth restored to its paradisiacal glory, the Savior, along with numerous resurrected Saints, such as Adam, Enoch, Abraham, Isaac, Jacob, Lehi, Nephi, Mormon, Moroni, and countless others will mingle with those on earth and teach them many things. How wonderful it will be to mingle with the righteous Saints from all dispensations of time—those who remained faithful to their covenants and thus merited a place in His Kingdom.

Thus there is much for those of our day to look forward too, not the doom and gloom that awaits the wicked, but the glories that await the righteous as the earth transcends from its current state to that of a terrestrial sphere. Thus, the prophesied coming of Christ should not strike fear in the hearts of man, but should bring joy at the prospects of the glories that await us.

Notes

1. Phyllis Carol Olive, "The Transfigured Earth," in *The Millennium: A Journey Through the Sabbath of Time* (Springville, UT: Bonneville Books, 2002), 71–82. Also, "Millennial Society," in *The Millennium: A Journey Through the Sabbath of Time*, 95–109.
2. Joseph Smith, *History of the Church*, 1:197.
3. John Taylor, in *Journal of Discourses*, 10:147.

16

Watch and Be Ready

Few can deny that evil powers, increasing in the United States, seek to control others by depriving them of their rights. Our Constitution is being shredded piece by piece, and our banking system is being effectively controlled by international bankers whose interests are not our own. Secret combinations are raging throughout the land just as they did during Book of Mormon times, disrupting the peace and the stability of our nation's financial and political institutions. The Lord was so concerned about their diabolical plots to destroy latter-day America that He commanded Moroni to include a warning about them on the gold plates for those of our day:

> 22 And whatsoever nation shall uphold such secret combinations, to get power and gain, until they shall spread over the nation, behold, they shall be destroyed; for the Lord will not suffer that the blood of his saints, which shall be shed by them, shall always cry unto him from the ground for vengeance upon them and yet he avenge them not.
>
> 24 Wherefore, the Lord commandeth you, when ye shall see these things come among you that ye shall awake to a sense of your awful situation, because of this secret combination which shall be among you; or wo be unto it, because of the blood of them who have been slain; for they cry from the dust for vengeance upon it, and also upon those who built it up.
>
> 26 Wherefore, I, Moroni, am commanded to write these things that evil may be done away, and that the time may come that Satan may have no power upon the hearts of the children of men, but that they

> may be persuaded to do good continually, that they may come unto the fountain of all righteousness and be saved. (Ether 8:22, 24, 26)

Secret Combinations and Communism

President Ezra Taft Benson describes Communism as a "gigantic conspiracy designed to enslave mankind."[1] In a conference address delivered on October 7, 1961, he spoke of the dangers that Communism posed to the United States. He said,

> Concerning the United States, the Lord revealed to his prophets that its greatest threat would be a vast, worldwide secret combination which would not only threaten the United States but seek to overthrow the freedom of all lands, nations, and countries. *In connection with the attack on the United States, the Lord told his prophet that there would be an attempt to overthrow the country by destroying the Constitution. . . .* The prophets in our day have continually warned us of these internal threats—that our greatest threat from Socialistic Communism lies within our country. . . . As the First Presidency pointed out in a statement signed in 1936, *if we continue to uphold Communism by not making it treasonable, our land shall be destroyed*, for the Lord has said that whatsoever nation shall uphold such secret combinations to get power and gain until they shall spread over the nation—behold, they shall be destroyed. *The Lord has declared that before the second coming of Christ, it will be necessary to destroy the secret works of darkness in order to preserve the land of Zion.*[2]

Our generation must be wary of designing men and women who wish to take away our freedoms. President Ezra Taft Benson also said,

> Because our forefathers—yours and mine—fought for the ideal of freedom, because our fathers preserved that ideal through our free competitive enterprise system under our God-given free agency, because they were willing to make religion the vital force of daily living, all of us have climbed through the years to new heights of well-being and inner strengths.
>
> But it is not only in the moral choice of right and wrong that man is free. Among the relentless quests of human history is the quest for political freedom. When the American patriot, Patrick Henry, shouted his immortal "Give me liberty or give me death," he did not speak idly. When at Philadelphia in 1776, the signers of the Declaration of

> Independence affixed their signatures to that sacred document, they, in a very real sense, were choosing liberty or death. . . .
>
> Yes, the founders of our country bequeathed to us a heritage of freedom and unity that is our most priceless political possession.[3]

Such a message is timely in any generation, yet it seems particularly timely in ours when much of our Constitution seems to be in peril of being abandoned or changed. President John Taylor said, "Besides the preaching of the Gospel, we have another mission, namely the perpetuation of the free agency of man and maintenance of liberty, freedom and the rights of man."[4] Nowhere else is this message given more poignantly than in the Book of Mormon, where we find the righteous Nephites fighting valiantly to keep their freedom against those who wanted a king—a state of affairs that would have cost them dearly.

Reading the Book of Mormon over and over again will bring such important messages to the forefront of our minds and keep us from making the same mistakes in our day—if only we will listen, for God has lost His patience. He said,

> 25 How oft have I called upon you by the mouth of my servants, and by the ministering of angels, and by mine own voice, and by the voice of thunderings, and by the voice of lightnings, and by the voice of tempests, and by the voice of earthquakes, and great hailstorms, and by the voice of famines and pestilences of every kind, and by the great sound of a trump, and by the voice of judgment, and by the voice of mercy all the day long, and by the voice of glory and honor and the riches of eternal life, and would have saved you with an everlasting salvation, but ye would not!
>
> 26 Behold, the day has come, when the cup of the wrath of mine indignation is full. (D&C 43:25–26)

A revolution is springing up by those who have been carefully and subtlety schooled in the ways of socialism over the past two or three decades. Some see this as a precursor to Communism. In a general priesthood session of general conference in April 1966, President David O. McKay said,

> The position of this Church on the subject of Communism has never changed. We consider it the greatest satanical threat to peace, prosperity, and the spread of God's work among men that exists on the face of the earth. . . .

> The entire concept and philosophy of Communism is diametrically opposed to everything for which the Church stands—belief in Deity, *belief in the dignity an eternal nature of man, and the application of the gospel to efforts for peace in the world.* Communism is militantly atheistic and is committed to the destruction of faith wherever it may be found.[5]

Our Prophets have often warned of possible warfare with Communistic countries, including China. Joseph Smith stated that "there is a land beyond the Rocky Mountains that will be invaded by the heathen Chinese unless great care and protection are given."[6] As far back as the 1930s, the Communists had a plan to take over America. Dmitri Z. Manuilsky said in a speech at the Lenin School of Political Warfare in Moscow,

> War to the hilt between Communism and Capitalism is inevitable. Today, of course, we are not strong enough to attack. Our time will come in 20 or 30 years. To win, we shall need the element of surprise, the bourgeoisie will have to be put to sleep.
>
> So we shall begin by launching the most spectacular peace movement on record. There will be electrifying overtures and unheard of concessions. The capitalist countries, stupid and decadent, will rejoice to cooperate in their own destruction. They will leap at another chance to be friends. A soon as their guard is down, we shall smash them with our clenched fists.[7]

So many prophecies refer to future periods of warfare that another war, or wars, in our future seems all but certain.

Plagues Accompany Warfare

Along with war and the destabilizing impact of earthquakes, tornadoes, famines, riots, and times of civil strife, plagues have also been prophesied to cleanse the earth in the last days. President John Taylor (an Apostle at the time) had a vision of the impending plague. He said that it was as though he was in the air looking down upon the terrible scenes before him. He said he saw a sign of mourning on every door in Salt Lake, and in every region north, south, east, and west of it. Washington, DC was a ghost town. The people had simply left the city, and left it to take care of itself. Dead bodies were piled up so high in Baltimore, Maryland, that they filled the town square. The waters of Chesapeake Bay were stagnant and filled with dead bodies. New York was also in ruins, and no signs of life could be found in Philadelphia. The entire states of Missouri and Illinois and part of Iowa were a complete wilderness.[8] Could this be the prophesied overflowing scourge and desolating sickness spoken of in latter-day prophecy?

> 31 And there shall be men standing in that generation, that shall not pass until they shall see an overflowing scourge; for a desolating sickness shall cover the land.
>
> 32 But my disciples shall stand in holy places, and shall not be moved; but among the wicked, men shall lift up their voices and curse God and die. (D&C 45:31–32)

Natural and Man-Made Disasters

Numerous scriptural references maintain that the Lord has simply had enough of the wickedness of man. Thus, major disasters in the form of famine, plagues, and warfare are destined to cleanse the earth of its wicked inhabitants prior to His Second Coming. President Benson said the following:

> Too often we bask in our comfortable complacency and rationalize that the ravages of war, economic disaster, famine, and earthquake cannot happen here. Those who believe this are either not acquainted with the revelations of the Lord, or they do not believe them. Those who smugly think these calamites will not happen, that they somehow will be set aside because of the righteousness of the Saints, are deceived and will rue the day they harbored such a delusion. The Lord has warned and forewarned us against a day of great tribulation and given us counsel, through His servants, on how we can be prepared for these difficult times. Have we heeded His counsel?[9]

Brigham Young said,

> "Do you think there is calamity abroad now among the people?" Not much. All we have yet heard and all we have experienced is scarcely a preface to the sermon that is going to be preached.
>
> When the testimony of the Elders ceases to be given, and the Lord says to them, "come home; I will now preach my own sermons to the nations of the earth," all you now know can scarcely be called a preface to the sermon that will be preached with fire and sword, tempests, earthquakes, hail, rain, thunders and lightnings, and fearful destruction. What matters the destruction of a few railway cars? You

> will hear of magnificent cities, now idolized by the people, sinking in the earth, entombing the inhabitants. The sea will heave itself beyond its bounds, engulphing *[sic]* mighty cities. Famine will spread over the nations, and nation will rise up against nation, kingdom against kingdom, and states against states, in our own country and in foreign lands; and they will destroy each other, caring not for the blood and lives of their neighbours, of their families, or for their own lives. They will be like the Jaredites who preceded the Nephites upon this continent, and will destroy each other to the last man, through the anger that the Devil will place in their hearts, because they have rejected the words of life and are given over to Satan to do whatever he listeth to do with them. You may think that the little you hear of now is grievous; yet the faithful of God's people will see days that will cause them to close their eyes because of the sorrow that will come upon the wicked nations. The hearts of the faithful will be filled with pain and anguish for them.[10]

Although the missionaries are still out in full force, America is already feeling what could be called the birth pains of preliminary disasters. Floods, tornadoes, and hurricanes descended upon the country with such fury in 2011 alone that thousands lost their homes, hundreds of people died, and much of America's farmlands were destroyed. As time goes by, such disasters are destined to increase until great multitudes of the wicked are swept from the land.

Be Ye Therefore Prepared

The First Presidency letter of 1988 urged the Saints to be prepared with enough basics to weather any emergency. It reads,

> We continue to encourage members to store sufficient food, clothing, and where possible fuel for at least one year. We have not laid down an exact formula for what should be stored. However, we suggest that members concentrate on essential foods that sustain life, such as grains, legumes, cooking oil, powdered milk, salt, sugar or honey, and water. Most families can achieve and maintain this basic level of preparedness. The decision to do more than this rests with the individual.
>
> We encourage you to follow this counsel with the assurance that a people prepared through obedience to the commandments of God need not fear.[11]

As early as 1857, Heber C. Kimball spoke of the need to store up food against a day of want, "Let us go to work and lay up our grain, lay up wheat, and everything that will and can be preserved; and in so doing, we will save ourselves from sorrow, pain and anguish; . . . wake up, ye Saints of the Most High, and prepare for any emergency that the Lord our God may have pleasure in bringing forth."[12]

The need to store food was emphasized again in a 1980 general conference where we heard, "The revelation to store food may be as essential to our temporal welfare today as boarding the ark was to the people in the days of Noah."[13] W. Don Ladd said in a general conference in 1994,

> We all need to build a personal ark. . . . And we shouldn't wait until it starts raining, but prepare in advance. This has been the message of all the prophets in this dispensation, . . . as well as the prophets of old.
>
> Unfortunately, we don't always heed the clear warnings of our prophets. We coast complacently along until calamity strikes, and then we panic.
>
> When it starts raining, it is too late to begin building the ark. However, we do need to listen to the Lord's spokesmen. We need to calmly continue to move ahead and prepare for what will surely come. We need not panic or fear, for if we are prepared, spiritually and temporally, we and our families will survive any flood. Our arks will float on a sea of faith if our works have been steadily and surely preparing for the future.[14]

Elder L. Tom Perry said, "As long as I can remember, we have been taught to prepare for the future and to obtain a year's supply of necessities. I would guess that the years of plenty have almost universally caused us to set aside this counsel. I believe the time to disregard this counsel is over. With events in the world today, it must be considered with all seriousness."[15]

President Spencer W. Kimball was troubled about the Saints seemingly lax response to such warnings, "We encourage families to have on hand this year's supply; and we say it over and over and over and repeat over and over the scripture of the Lord where He says, "Why call ye me Lord, Lord, and do not the things which I say?" [Luke 6:46]. How empty it is as they put their spirituality, so-called, into action and call him by his important names, but fail to do the things which he says?"[16]

In anticipation of a likely disruption in our monetary system in the near future, we are also advised to have a year's supply of other necessities. President Benson suggests that after we store food, we should also "store . . . clothing and fuel." If we are faithful to that duty, he tells us, "You will not be confronted with the danger of losing all you have because of inflation or depression. You will have security that no government can provide—savings and supplies for emergencies."[17]

He continued, "It is well to remember that continued government deficits cause inflation; inflation is used as an excuse for ineffective price controls; price controls lead to shortages; artificial shortages inevitably are used as an excuse to implement rationing. When will we learn these basic economic principles?"[18]

President J. Reuben Clark Jr. said, "Where food is scare or there is none at all, and so with clothing and shelter, money may be no good for there may be nothing to buy, and you cannot eat money, you cannot get enough of it together to burn to keep warm, and you cannot wear it."[19]

President Gordon B. Hinckley foresaw the danger of an economic meltdown of world markets in 1998 when he spoke to the boys and men in general conference about the stormy weather ahead:

> There is a portent of stormy weather ahead to which we had better give heed. . . .
>
> No one knows when emergencies will strike. . . . Set your houses in order. If you have paid your debts, if you have a reserve, even though it be small, then should storms howl about your head, you will have shelter for your wives and children and peace in your hearts. That's all I have to say about it, but I wish to say it with all the emphasis of which I am capable.[20]

In 2008, the financial markets in America took a nosedive—perhaps a precursor to an even greater global event. As to when the various disasters are destined to strike, Elder Bruce R. McConkie said,

> We do not know when the calamities and troubles of the last days will fall upon any of us as individuals or upon bodies of the Saints. The Lord deliberately withholds from us the day and hour of his coming and the tribulations which shall precede it—all as part of the testing and probationary experiences of mortality. He simply tells us to watch and be ready.
>
> We can rest assured that if we have done all in our power to prepare for whatever lies ahead, he will then help us with whatever else we need.
>
> He rained manna from heaven upon all Israel, six days each week for forty years, lest they perish for want of bread. . . [Exodus 16:3–4].
>
> During forty years in the wilderness the clothes worn by all Israel waxed not old and their shoe wore not out. . . . [Deuteronomy 29:5].

> When there was a famine in the land, at Elijah's word, a certain barrel of meal did not waste and a certain cruze of oil did not fail, until the Lord sent again rain on the earth. And it is worthy of note, as Jesus said, that though there were many widows in Israel, unto only one was Elijah sent [1 Kings 17:10–16].
>
> We do not say that all of the Saints will be spared and saved from the coming day of desolation. But we do say there is no promise of safety and no promise of security except for those who love the Lord and who are seeking to do all that he commands.[21]

According to various latter-day prophets, the calamites we have witnessed in our day are but a prelude to the sermons that the Lord will yet preach, while He cleanses His vineyard before His Second Coming to rule as King of kings during a thousand years of peace. Thus, the leaders of the Church have continually encouraged the Saints to move quietly along in their preparations to meet the storms when they come. Unfortunately, far too few of the Saints are heeding the council to prepare, just as many people did during Noah's day. For that reason, the First Presidency issued a new letter in 2002, instructing all Priesthood and Relief Society leaders around the world to encourage their members to store at least a year's supply of food and necessities, so they can ride out the disasters which have already begun to fall upon the nations.[22]

God Is at the Helm

There can be little doubt that the winding-up scene of this earth's temporal existence is happening before our very eyes, with many around us crying doom and gloom so loudly that we can scarcely keep from slipping into a deep depression. Despair seems to fill our thoughts continually, and we sometimes lose hope of any future happiness. We are watching our once great nation crumble under the weight of lawlessness. Neighborhoods that were once safe havens for our people have turned into crime-ridden ghettos. Children who used to play in playgrounds now gather in gangs and revel in destructive behavior. The innocence of entertainment has become eroded to the point where it is a breeding ground for evil delights of every kind. Music that once flowed gently through our homes now jangles our nerves and offers lyrics not suitable to hear. Politicians serve their own needs instead of that of the nation, and the news media is so quick to twist the events of the day for ratings that we don't know who we can trust anymore. Unfortunately, the wickedness of a people brings with it the withdrawal of the Spirit of the Lord, leaving Lucifer free to rule the land.

Sadly, we are seeing only the beginning of the woes yet to come. Prophecies tell us that wickedness will worsen until the world is ripe for destruction. Yet it will be the wicked, not the righteous, who are doomed. Whatever means the Lord chooses to destroy the ungodly, we must trust that that the righteous will be spared. Thus, we must not fear or wallow in despair. Yet, that is a difficult thing to ask of us. How can we not fear when we look at the countries of the world that are crumbing all around us while millions of people are either being slaughtered or driven from their homes with little more than the clothes on their backs? How can we not fear when we know from past experience that when a nation becomes as wicked as ours has, the Spirit of God withdraws? We can feel it, and we can see the fruits of that withdrawal as men's hearts harden all around us, and evil seems to be winning. Millions of babies are being slaughtered through abortion worldwide, drugs have enslaved millions more, and bigotry and racism are rampant. The news media stops at nothing to bring us every piece of dirt or horror they can find to greet us every morning when we first wake up, and then on and on until we fall into a fretful sleep at night.

But we must pause here, and remember that God is at the helm and is winning in this fight for the souls of men. While the battle between good and evil continues to escalate, we must remember that this is God's war, not ours, and His strategies are not always ours to understand. When the time comes that disasters strike, or evil presents itself at our doors, we must pray for guidance and strength, and legions of heavenly hosts will be there to preserve our righteous families. Trust in His arm; trust in His promise that the righteous need not fear if they are prepared physical, spiritually, and temporally. Let God direct His work in His own way, and in His own good time.

Today, God's army of Latter-day missionaries are scouring the earth in search of the righteous and pure in heart. Their task is to go to all the world and gather in the lost sheep of Israel and plant them in the pastures of Zion. Then, and only then will God reap the whirlwind and destroy the wicked from off the face of the earth. God is at the helm, make no mistake about it, and if we stand in holy places in the stakes of Zion, we should not fear.

Reflections

Each year at its close, just before New Year's Day, we reflect on the news of the year. Each TV network presents a short clip of all of the previous year's bad news; it passes quickly before eyes as we sit in horror and wonder how we survived it all. Yet, during that year, babies were born, marriages took place, we went to school and to work, and we laughed and cried and played. We worked in the garden and perhaps went on trips or vacations. We enjoyed Christmas and holidays; we bought new clothes or cars or toys and enjoyed them. We enjoyed our pets and painted the house. We were sick and we got well. We changed jobs or went to college or retired. We visited relatives and went through the death and burials of loved ones—in other words, life went on.

There will be times when we are called upon to defend our homes and families against the forces of evil in a very real sense. When that day comes, do so with an eye single to the admonition to defend, not to reap vengeance and indulge in the kind of hatred that turns our hearts cold. Remember, that vengeance is the Lord's, and this is His war. God knows what He is doing and will preserve our great country, if only for the sake of the righteous. Thus, let our countenances be fixed on that time when the Savior completes His messy cleanup, and peace reigns supreme for a thousand years. Until that day, we must strengthen our families and prepare ourselves spiritually, physically, and intellectually. We must follow the counsel of the Brethren to read our scriptures daily lest we be swept away with every whim and doctrine that blows in the wind, or that pleases the senses. Pray daily that you may build a relationship with your Father in Heaven and be the recipient of His Holy Spirit, so that it can guide your actions and help you discern between good and evil. Strengthen your families through prayer and family home evening, and claim the promises given that if you are faithful in this charge your little ones will grow up in the faith.

It might also be wise to choose the simplest means of keeping abreast of current events without allowing the news media to totally engulf your life with the horrors of the world on a minute-by-minute basis. No one can carry the burden of a warring world on their shoulders for long without buckling under the weight of it all. How grateful I am for the Prophet Mormon who left off telling us in too much detail about the atrocities the wicked were inflicting upon on the righteous during the final battle of the Nephites, lest our tender hearts be broken (see Mormon 5:9). Follow that admonition today. Be informed and well-read, but not to the point where your lives are bogged down in a perpetual mire of sadness and despair. Go about your lives with your minds fixed solidly on the fact that whatever happens in this war-torn world, God is at the helm and will direct things as he sees fit. He will inform His prophets of any change in course that the Saints need to take for their continued care and safety. Walk in faith, knowing that the Lord will lead the righteous to places of security before disaster hits. This should ease the minds of the pure in heart, who can then look forward with joyful anticipation for the prophesied coming of Christ. This is a glorious time to live—a time when the prophecies of the coming of Christ are unfolding before our very eyes.

Notes

1. Ezra Taft Benson, *An Enemy Hath Done This*, compiled by Jerrald L. Newquist (Salt Lake City: Parliament Publishers, 1969), 110.
2. Duane S. Crowther, *Prophecy: Key to the Future* (Bountiful, UT: Horizon Publishers, 1962), 11; italics in original.
3. Ezra Taft Benson, *An Enemy Hath Done This*, compiled by Jerrald L. Newquist (Salt Lake City: Parliament Publishers, 1969), 17.
4. John Taylor, in *Journal of Discourses*, 23:63.
5. David O. McKay, in *Conference Report*, April 1966, 109–10; italics in original.
6. Duane S. Crowther, *Prophecy: Key to the Future* (Bountiful, UT: Horizon Publishers, 1962), 13.
7. "As Manuilsky Was Saying . . . ," *The Ukrainian Weekly*, September 17, 1960, accessed March 20, 2017, ukrweekly.com/old/archive/1960/1796021.shtml.

8. W. Cleon Skousen, *The Cleansing of America* (Valor Publishing, 2010), 14–15.

9. Ezra Taft Benson, *The Teachings of Ezra Taft Benson* (Salt Lake City: Bookcraft, 1988), 706.

10. Brigham Young, in *Journal of Discourses*, 8:123.

11. "Preparing for Emergencies," Letter from the First Presidency, June 24, 1988.

12. Heber C. Kimball, in *Journal of Discourses*, 5:163–64.

13. Ezra Taft Benson, "Prepare for the Days of Tribulation," *Ensign*, November 1980.

14. W. Don Ladd, " 'Make Thee an Ark'," *Ensign*, November 1994.

15. L. Tom Perry, " 'If Ye Are Prepared Ye Shall Not Fear'," *Ensign*, November 1985.

16. Spencer W. Kimball, "Family Preparedness," *Ensign*, May 1976.

17. Benson, *The Teachings of Ezra Taft Benson*, 263.

18. Ibid., 268.

19. J. Reuben Clark Jr., *Church News* (November 21, 1953), 4. See also Benson, *The Teachings of Ezra Taft Benson*, 268.

20. Gordon B. Hinckley, "To the Boys and to the Men," *Ensign* November 1998.

21. Bruce R. McConkie, "Stand Independent above All Other Creatures," *Ensign*, May 1979.

22. "Letter from the First Presidency," *Liahona*, April 2003.

Bibliography

Anderson, Mad Bear. "The Peacemaker's Prophecy." *Earth Mother Crying.* earthmothercrying.org/iroquoisprophecy.htm.

"As Manuilsky Was Saying . . . ." *The Ukrainian Weekly.* ukrweekly.com /old/archive/1960/1796021.shtml.

Baldwin, John D. *Ancient America in Notes on American Archaeology.* CreateSpace, 2015.

Ballard, Timothy. *The Covenant: One Nation Under God.* New York: Legends Library, 2012.

Balmforth, David N. *America's Coming Crisis: Prophetic Warings, Divine Destiny.* Bountiful UT: Horizon Publishers, 1998.

Bancroft, Hubert Howe. *The Works of Hubert Howe Bancroft: The Native Races.* San Francisco: A. L. Bancroft and Company, 1883.

Benson, Ezra Taft. *An Enemy Hath Done This.* Compiled by Jerreld L. Newquist. Salt Lake City: Parliament Publishers, 1969.

———. "Our Divine Constitution." *Ensign,* November 1987.

———. "Prepare for the Days of Tribulation." *Ensign,* November 1980.

———. *The Teachings of Ezra Taft Benson.* Salt Lake City: Bookcraft, 1988.

Berta, Christine. "Biography: St. Thomas the Apostle." *St. Thomas the Apostle Catholic Church*. www.stapostle.org/st-thomas-church-parish-history/saint-thomas-biography/.

Book of Jasher. Salt Lake City: J. H. Parry & Company, 2007.

Britannica Encyclopedia of World Religions. "Handsome Lake Movement."

britjas. "Observations from the Navajo Nation." *LDS Freedom Forum*. www.ldsfreedomforum.com/viewtopic.php?t=9492.

Burke, George Abbot. "The Apostle of India." *Original Christianity and Original Yoga*. ocoy.org/original-christianity/apostle-of-india/.

Cannon, Donald Q. "Zelph Revisited." emp.byu.edu/marrottr/341folder/zelph%20%revisit%20cannon.html.

"Cherokee Prophecies." *Crystalinks*. www.crystalinks.com/cherokeeprophecy.html.

Clark, J. Reuben, Jr. *Church News*. November 21, 1953.

Conoly, Rebecca, and Russell Grigg. "Flood." *Creation.com*. October 12, 2011, creation.com/many-flood-legends#txtRef9.

Crowther, Duane S. *Prophecy: Key to the Future*. Bountiful, UT: Horizon Publishers, 1997.

Dostou, Tom. "Seven Fires Prophecy of the Anishnabe People and the Process of Reconciliation." *Prayer Vigil for the Earth*. oneprayer.org/SevenFiresProphecyAnishnabePeople.html.

Dragoo, Don W. In *Hopewellian Studies*. Edited by Joseph R. Caldwell and Robert L. Hall. Springfield, IL: Illinois State Museum, 1970.

Fell, Barry. *America B. C.: Ancient Settlers in the New World*. Muskogee, OK: Artisan Publishers, 1989.

French, Ellen and Richard C. Hanes. "Hopis." *Countries and Their Cultures*. www.everyculture.com/multi/Ha-La/Hopis.html.

Frykenberg, Robert Eric. *Christianity in India: From Beginnings to the Present*. Oxford: Oxford University Press, 2008.

Godfrey, Kenneth W. "What Is the Significance of Zelph in the Study of Book of Mormon Geography?" *Journal of Book of Mormon Studies* 8, no. 2 (1999).

Glossary of Indian Nations. www.hotcakencyclopedia.com/ho .GlossaryIndianNations.html.

Gordon, Cyrus. *Before Columbus: Links between the Old World and Ancient America*. Crown Pub, 1971.

Gordon, E. O. *Prehistoric London: Its Mounds and Circles*. Fourth edition. London: Covenant Publishing, 1946.

Guirand, Felix. *The Larousse Encyclopedia of Mythology*. London: Chancellor Press, 1996.

Hale, Horatio. "Hiawatha and the Iroquois Confederation." *Mark Shepard's Peace Page*. www.markshep.com/peace/Hiawatha.html.

Hansen, L. Taylor. *He Walked the Americas.* Amherst WI: Legend Press, 1994.

Hinckley, Gordon B. "To the Boys and to the Men." *Ensign* November 1998.

"Hopi Prophecies." *Crystalinks.*, www.crystalinks.com/hopi2.html

Imparto, Edward T., comp. *General MacArthur: Wisdom and Visions.* Kentucky: Turner Publishing, 2000.

Jackson, Jerry. "Overcoming Illiteracy: God's Word and Lasting Fruit." *Lausanne World Pulse Archives*, no. 7, (2009). www .lausanneworldpulse.com/themedarticles-php/1164/07-2009.

Jessee, Dean C., ed. *The Papers of Joseph Smith*. Salt Lake City: Deseret Book, 2008.

"John Cabot." *Royal Museums Greenwich*. www.rmg.co.uk/discover /explore/john-cabot.

Journal of Discourses. 26 vols. London: Latter-day Saints' Book Depot, 1854–86.

Journal of Wilford Woodruff. April 6, 1837.

Jowett, George F. *The Drama of the Lost Disciples*. Covenant Publishing, 2001.

Khan, Annie. "Interpretation of Ancient Navajo Chants." *Prophecy Fulfilled.* prophecy-fulfilled.com/navajo.htm.

Kimball, Spencer W. "Family Preparedness." *Ensign*, May 1976.

———. *Teachings of Spencer W. Kimball.* Salt Lake City: The Church of Jesus Christ of Latter-day Saints, 2012.

Ladd, Don W. "'Make Thee an Ark'." *Ensign*, November 1994.

Lee, Harold B. "The Spirit of Gathering" *Improvement Era*, May 1948.

"Letter from the First Presidency." *Liahona*, April 2003.

Lopez, Antonio. *From the Roof of the World to the Land of Enchantment: The Tibet-Pueblo Connection.* In Tibet Diary. "Links/Similiarities between Tibetan and Native America Groups." *Tibetalk.* tibettalk.wordpress.com/2007/11/01/linkssimilarities-between-tibetan-and-native-american-groups/.

Lund, Gerald N. *The Coming of the Lord.* Salt Lake City: Bookcraft, 2002.

Malhi, Ripan S., Beth A. Schultx, and David Glenn Smith. "Distribution of Mitochondrial DNA Lineages among Native American Tribes of Northeastern North America." *Human Biology* 73, no. 1, (February 2001). doi:10.1353/hub.2001.0008.

Martin, Ken. "Legend of the Keetoowah." *Manataka American Indian Council.* www.manataka.org/page275.html.

Masonic Dictionary Online. "Crosses." www.masonicdictionary.com/crosses.html.

———. "Tau." www.masonicdictionary.com/tau.html.

"Masons (Freemasonry): Christian or Anti-Christian?" *rapidnet.com.* rapidnet.com/~jbeard/bdm/Cults/masons.htm.

Matlock, Gene. *India Once Ruled the Americas!* Lincoln, NE: iUniverse, 2000.

McConkie, Bruce R. "Stand Independent above All Other Creatures." *Ensign*, May 1979.

McGavin, E. Cecil, and Willard Bean. *The Geography of the Book of Mormon.* Second edition. Salt Lake City: Bookcraft, 1949.

McIntosh, John. *The Origin of North American Indians; with a Faithful Description of Their Manners and Customs, Both Civil and Military, Their Religions, Languages, Dress, and Ornaments . . . .* New York: Nafish & Cornish, 1849.

McKay, David O. In *Conference Report*, April 1966.

Murphree, Daniel S., ed. *Native America: A State-by-State Historical Encyclopedia*. Vol. 1, *Alabama–Louisiana*. Santa Barbara, CA: Greenwood, 2012.

Mythologies: A Polytheistic View of the World. PediaPress.

Nequatewa, Edmund. "Dr. Fewkes and Masauwu." *The South Corner of Time*. parentseyes.arizona.edu/southcorner/hopi_drfewkes.html.

Nibley, Hugh. *Enoch the Prophet*. Salt Lake City: Deseret Book, 1986.

———. *Teachings of the Book of Mormon*. Lecture 60. In "The Ancient and the Academic: Hugh Nibley's Teaching, Dealings and Understanding of the Hopi." Jody Livingston. *Book of Mormon Archaeological Forum*. www.bmaf.org/node/451.

Ojibwa. "Mormon Missionaries and the Hopi Indians." *Native American Netroots*. nativeamericannetroots.net/diary/758.

Olive, Phyllis Carol. *The Lost Lands of the Book of Mormon*. Springville, UT: Cedar Fort, 2012.

———. *The Lost Sheep of Ancient America: Bringing the Lands and People of the Book of Mormon to Life*. Springville, UT: Cedar Fort, Inc., 2015.

———. *The Millennium: A Journey Through the Sabbath of Time.* Springville, UT: Bonneville Books, 2002.

"Original Inhabitants of the 13 Colonies." *United States History*. www.u-s-history.com/pages/h936.html.

Parker, Arthur C. "The Code of Handsome Lake, the Seneca Prophet." *Internet Sacred Text Archive*. www.sacred-texts.com/nam/iro/parker/index.htm.

Perry, L. Tom. " 'If Ye Are Prepared Ye Shall Not Fear'." *Ensign*, November 1985.

Peterson, Daniel C. *The Last Day: Teachings of the Modern Prophets*. Aspen Books, 1998.

Pound, Roscoe. *Lectures on Masonic Jurisprudence.* Little Masonic Library, no. 4. Macoy Publishing, 1977. In "Masons (Freemasonry): Christian or Anti-Christian?" *rapidnet.com*. rapidnet.com/~jbeard/bdm/Cults/masons.htm.

"Preparing for Emergencies." Letter from the First Presidency. June 24, 1988.

"Proclamation of the Twelve Apostles of The Church of Jesus Christ of Latter-day Saints." *Millennial Star*. April 6, 1845.

"Quetzalcoatl: Man or Myth?" *123helpme!.com.* 123helpme.com/view .asp?id=82876.

"Red Elk's Version of Deganawidah." *Earth Mother Crying*. earthmothercrying.org/iroquoisprophecy.htm.

Redfern, Gayle. *Ancient Wisdoms: Exploring the Mysteries and Connections.* Bloomington, IN: AuthorHouse, 2009.

Reidla, Maere, Toomas Kivisild, Ene Metspalu, Katrin Kaldma, Kristiina Tambets, Helle-Viivi Tolk, Jüri Parik et. al. "Origin and Diffusion of mtDNA haplogroup X." *The American Journal of Human Genetics* 73, (2003). doi:10.1086/379380.

Ritchie, William A. *The Archaeology of New York State*. Revised edition. New York: Natural History Press, 1997.

Roberts, B. H. *History of the Church*. 7 vols.

———. *New Witnesses for God: The Book of Mormon.* Salt Lake City: Deseret News, 1951.

Romney, Marion G. "America's Destiny." *Ensign*, November 1975.

Schmal, John P. "Are You Related to the Aztecs?: Uto-Aztecan Languages Spoken Throughout Mexico and the Western United States." *Traditions of Mexico*. www.houstonculture.org/mexico/aztec .html.

"Siouan Migrations and Iroquois Conquests." *Access Genealogy*. www .accessgenealogy.com/native/siouan-migrations-and-iroquois -conquests.htm.

Skousen W. Cleon. *The Cleansing of America*. Valor Publishing, 2010.

———. *The First 2000 Years*. Salt Lake City: Bookcraft, 1953.

Smith, Joseph Fielding. In *Conference Report*. April 1937.

———. *Doctrines of Salvation*, Compiled by Bruce R. McConkie. Salt Lake City: Bookcraft, 1992.

———., arr. *Teachings of the Prophet Joseph Smith*. Third edition. Salt Lake City: Deseret News Press, 1942.

Sun Bear with Wabun Wind. *Black Dawn, Bright Day: Indian Prophecies for the Millennium That Reveal the Fate of the Earth*. New York: Simon & Schuster, 1992.

"Tibet, Tibet." *Martine & Stephen Batchelor*. www.stephenbatchelor.org /index.php/en/tibet-tibet.

"Tree of Peace and Caduceus." *dyarrow.org*. www.dyarrow.org/indigenous /caduseus.htm.

Veytia, Mariano. *Ancient America Rediscovered*. Compiled by Donald W. Hemingway and W. David Hemingway. Springville UT: Bonneville Books, 2000.

Waldman, Carl. *Encyclopedia of Native American Tribes*. Revised edition. New York: Checkmark Books, 1999.

Warren, William. *History of the Ojibway People*. Minnesota Historical Society Press, 1984.

Waters, Frank. *Book of the Hopi*. New York: Penguin Books, 1977.

Whitney, Orson F. *The Life of Heber C. Kimball*. Salt Lake City: Bookcraft, 1973.

"Who Were the Essenes?" *Essene Spirit*. essenespirit.com/who.html.

Wikipedia. "Boko Haran." en.wikipedia.org/wiki/Boko_Haram.

———. "Catawba people." en.wikipedia.org/wiki/Catawba_people.

———. "Great Peacemaker." en.wikipedia.org/wiki/Great_Peacemaker.

———. "Hopi mythology." en.wikipedia.org/wiki/Hopi_mythology.

———. "Indian Removal Act." en.wikipedia.org/wiki/Indian_Removal _Act.

———. "Padmasambhava." en.wikipedia.org/wiki/Padmasambhava.

———. "Proto-Algonquian language." en.wikipedia.org/wiki/Proto -Algonquian_language.

———. "Saint Thomas Christians." en.wikipedia.org/wiki/Saint _Thomas_Christians.

———. "Seven fires prophecy." en.wikipedia.org/wiki/Seven_fires _prophecy.

Williams, Samuel Cole. *Adair's History of the American Indians.* New York: Promontory Press, 1986.

Woodruff, Wilford. In *Conference Report.* April 1898.

Yarrow, David. "The Great Law of Peace: New World Roots of American Democracy." *dyarrow.org.* www.dyarrow.org/indigenous/greatlaw.htm.

Yorgason, Blaine and Brenton. *Spiritual Survival in the Last Days.* Salt Lake City: Deseret Book, 1990.

Other Books by Phyllis Carol Olive

The Lost Lands of the Book of Mormon: A Geographical and Historical Study of the Book of Mormon Using the New York Setting at a Time When Primeval Forests and Ancient Waters Filled the Land

The Lost Tribes of the Book of Mormon: The Rest of the Story; A Correlation between the Nephite Nation and the Mound Builders of the Eastern United States

The Lost Sheep of Ancient America: Bringing the Lands and People of the Book of Mormon to Life

The Lost Empires and Vanished Races of the Book of Mormon

The Millennium: A Journey through the Sabbath of Time

The Holy Ghost

Baptism: The Key to Heaven

About the Author

Phyllis Carol Olive, author of the best-selling book *The Lost Lands of the Book of Mormon* and its sequel, *The Lost Tribes of the Book of Mormon*, lives in Las Vegas, Nevada, with her husband, Ron Olive.

She is a passionate researcher of the New York setting for the Book of Mormon, and her research has culminated in several other books, including *The Lost Empires and Vanished Races of the Book of Mormon*, *The Lost Sheep of Ancient America*, and her latest book, *The Prophesied Coming of Christ.*

Her website, bookofmormonlands.com, contains several videos dedicated to Book of Mormon geography and its place near New York's Hill Cumorah.

Scan to visit

www.bookofmormonlands.com